Mind-Reading Card Tricks

ROBERT MANDELBERG

Illustrated by Ferruccio Sardella

D0111427

STERLING PUBLISHING CO., INC.
New York

This book would have been really bad, if Nika, my wife, had not told me to take out a certain part. I reread the part in question, and she was right. It wasn't so good. So I dedicate this Book to Nika, the woman who single-handedly pointed out that a certain part of the book needed to be changed.

Thank you:

To Joel Lerner for great banter and the secret behind *What's Your Number?*

To Rodman: He reads, he contemplates, he punctuates. His middle name is Pilgrim.

OTHER BOOKS BY ROBERT MANDELBERG

The Case of the Curious Campaign:
A Whodunit of Many Mini-Mysteries

Mystifying Mind Reading Tricks

Library of Congress Cataloging-in-Publication Data

Mandelberg, Robert.
    Mind-reading card tricks / Robert Mandelberg ; illustrated by Ferruccio Sardella.
        p. cm.
    Includes index.
    Summary: Explains how to perform card tricks, from warm-ups to feature demonstrations, each "chosen for its ability to leave audiences stupefied" and relying on the magician's ability to convince the audience of his or her psychic powers.
    ISBN 1-4027-0948-X
    1. Card tricks--Juvenile literature. 2. Telepathy--Juvenile literature. [1. Card tricks. 2. Telepathy.] I. Sardella, Ferruccio, ill. II. Title.
GV1549.M26 2004
793.8'5--dc22

                                                                                  2003022668

Diagram Art (pp. 42, 43, 54, 60, 66) by Robert Steimle
Edited and Layout by Rodman Pilgrim Neumann

4   6   8   10   9   7   5

Published by Sterling Publishing Co., Inc.
387 Park Avenue South, New York, NY 10016
© 2004 by Robert Mandelberg
Distributed in Canada by Sterling Publishing
^{c}/o Canadian Manda Group, 165 Dufferin Street,
Toronto, Ontario, Canada M6K 3H6
Distributed in Great Britain and Europe by Chris Lloyd at Orca Book
Services, Stanley House, Fleets Lane, Poole BH15 3AJ, England
Distributed in Australia by Capricorn Link (Australia) Pty. Ltd.
P.O. Box 704, Windsor, NSW 2756, Australia

Sterling ISBN 1-4027-0948-X

For information about custom editions, special sales, premium and corporate purchases, please contact Sterling Special Sales Department at 800-805-5489 or specialsales@sterlingpub.com.

Contents

Introduction 5

1. Mind Reading: Fact or Fiction 7

2. It's All in the Presentation 13

3. One Up 17

4. Behind the Back 22

5. Under the Table 25

6. The Envelope, Please 29

7. Seven Up 33

8. How Did I Do That? 41

9. Psychic-in-Training 51

10. Switcheroo! 56

11. What's Your Number? 64

12. Telepathy for Two 72

13. Spellbound 82

14. Neighborhood ESP 88

Index 95

Introduction

When it comes right down to it, I don't think that people enjoy seeing card tricks. Do you? Is it fun when the magician tricks you into believing he guessed the correct card, or miraculously produces your card—a three of spades—from a sealed envelope inside a locked safe buried two miles beneath the Atlantic Ocean?

Of course it isn't fun. It's frustrating, confusing, and—most of all—maddening. Oh, and the worst part is that wisecracking magician, so pleased with himself, looking smug and smiling condescendingly. And the way the spectators fawn all over him; it's disgusting! "Oh, Mr. Magician, you're so clever; oh, Mr. Magician, how did you do that?; oh, Mr. Magician, do that again!"

Mr. Magician, Mr. Magician, ha! Enough already. I think if the general public rated the type of people they hated the most, magicians would be right up there with criminals, line cutters, and cheese salesmen. No, people do not enjoy card tricks or the people who perform them.

On the other hand, it is quite another story if *you're* the magician. Yes, you see, if you're the one guessing the cards, predicting the future, and pulling threes and sevens from the Atlantic Ocean, then life has quite a different meaning. All of a sudden it's *you* who are the hit of the party; *you* who know the answer to what everyone wants to know;

you who are standing smug and confident, watching your soon-to-be ex-friends begging to find out *how did you do that?*

Yes, it is true: being the magician is far better than being the spectator. Anyone will tell you that. It's common sense. I, for one, would much rather be a wolf than a deer, a spider than a fly, and, more poetically, as the immortal Paul Simon once said, *"I'd rather be a hammer than a nail."* If you have a choice, reader—and you do—pick magician over spectator. You'll thank me for it.

That is where this book comes in. In these pages, you will find the answers to the most devastating and mild-blowing card tricks ever created. And this is not just my opinion. *It's fact.*

These jolting feats are so powerful because they will call upon you to use your "mind reading talents." Sure, any amateur magician can pull a fast one and make the four of clubs appear at the top of the deck, but how many can *predict* cards chosen by spectators? How many of these so-called magicians can appear to transmit mental vibes to people thousands of miles away—across continents even—to accurately predict a card that's been selected? Not many.

What you are about to read is a collection of mind-reading card tricks that have been researched, hand-selected, improved, or invented by this author. I have limited this selection to just top-tier demonstrations, ranging from simple warm-ups to high-impact, mind-blowing, run-down-the-street-screaming miracles. Each one has been chosen for its ability to leave audiences stupefied. These card tricks were designed to actually cause mental and emotional damage to the spectators witnessing them. They are so *horrifying* that people have been known to spontaneously combust upon witnessing them. In fact, this book should not even be in the magic section; its proper home is alongside the Steven King novels because of the sheer terror it will wreak.

Sirs and madams, if you have any decency in you, I implore you to put this book down and pick up something more civil, such as *Home Decorating Tips by Nika.* But if decency is not among your better attributes, then discreetly buy this book, bring it to your lair, and begin to learn some of the diabolical secrets of mind reading. Don't say I didn't warn you!

— Robert Mandelberg

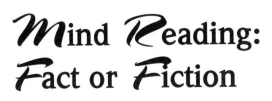

*M*ind *R*eading: *F*act or *F*iction

I hate to be the one to break it to you, but it is not possible to read someone's mind. No matter how much we try, we will never be able to know what is going on inside someone else's head. And why would we want to? We have enough trouble keeping track of the goings-on in our own heads without having to worry about someone else's twisted thoughts.

Millions of dollars are spent every year on crystal balls, tarot cards, psychics, Magic 8 Balls, and other sources in an attempt to read minds and predict the future. With the exception of the Magic 8 Ball, none of these methods has proven to be the slightest bit effective. Neither will this book, I am afraid.

But . . . if you would like to *appear* as if you can read minds; if you want people to *think* that you have psychic powers; if you want to see the look of awe in your friends' eyes as you perform impossible feats of mentalism, then I think I can be of some assistance. With the aid of ordinary playing cards, this book will teach you how to perform some of the most stunning and earth-shattering mind-reading feats ever conceived.

Pillars of Mind Reading

Let's reach an understanding. If you want to give the impression that you have psychic powers, then you are going to have to resort to trickery. Oh, don't act so shocked. How did you think you were going to mind read? By squeezing your eyes tight and going into a trance? Please. I have a feeling that if you could do that, you would not be reading this book.

So, trickery it is. And since you will be resorting to methods that upstanding, decent citizens might consider sneaky and underhanded, you must be discreet and learn to hide your deceptions. Don't worry; I won't make you do it alone. I will be right by your side with hints and step-by-step instructions to minimize the risk of getting caught. In addition to showing you the solution to seemingly impossible mind reading feats, I will also provide insider tips and performance suggestions to leave your audiences bewildered and entertained.

And it's not as if these skills won't come in handy time and again. You will see how much of a demand there is in today's competitive job market for people who can guess cards that other people have picked from a deck. It is an excellent qualification to include on your résumé.

Although there are countless variations, the secrets to most mind reading card demonstrations can be broken down into seven basic techniques. Let's examine them briefly.

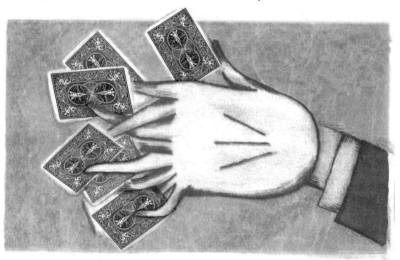

SLEIGHT OF HAND

Many superb mind reading exhibitions are made possible through sly maneuvers while the audience is distracted. These include false shuffles, switched decks, sneaky dealing, card palming, and general trickery. It's the old "hand is quicker than the eye" routine. The demos described in this book that use sleight of hand are simple and require only a few minutes of practice to master.

FORCING A CARD

Free will? When it comes to "pick a card, any card," there's no such thing. There are numerous methods you could use to influence a spectator's selection when he is "choosing" a card from the deck. Although this is a valid technique in mind reading, many of the moves require highly developed card handling skills or use mathematical formulas to achieve results. I have included one demonstration (*Seven Up*, see Chapter 7) that uses this method because the force is simple and the payoff is usually spectacular.

FALSE ASSUMPTION

One of the chief functions of the mind reader is to mislead the observers into believing a false premise. If he is successful, the audience is ripe for being fooled. Here is an example of a simple trick that uses false assumptions:

Two-Faced

Start with an ordinary deck of cards and turn the bottom card over. Now, both the bottom and top of the deck have cards that are showing their backs. Fan out the cards facedown in your hands and ask a spectator to select one. While she is looking at her card, secretly turn the deck upside down.

Now hold the deck in a stack and ask her to replace the card in the deck anywhere she wants. She can only see the top card and will *assume* that all cards are facedown—when in fact, only the top card is facedown. With this false assumption, she will replace the card facedown, making it easy for you to identify her card in the deck.

This technique is similar to the one used in *Under the Table* described in Chapter 5.

PRESET DECK

Here is a daring technique that opens the door to a whole new world of deception and trickery for a mind reader. This method, however, sometimes rouses the suspicions of the audience. Spectators are usually on the lookout for pre-arranged cards, and feel more comfortable if they are allowed to shuffle and cut the deck. As you will see in the coming chapters, there are ways you can use preset decks that still allow the audience to mix the cards completely.

9

Here is an example of a basic demonstration that uses a preset deck:

Double Decker

Secretly preset the deck by separating the red cards from the black cards. Place them in two piles facedown on a table. While telling the audience that this demonstration uses only half the deck, grab the red cards and fan them out facedown. Ask a spectator to select a card and show everyone what it is (excluding you). While they are looking at the card, discreetly put down the red cards on the table and pick up the black half. Ask the spectator to replace the card anywhere in the deck. When you look at the cards, you will see only one red card mixed in with all black cards. Easy, and so effective.

EVIL MATHEMATICS

How could something as wholesome and pure as mathematics be so dastardly and downright devious? Mathematics used to be a friendly companion, always there to help figure out equations, calculate correct change, and determine how many two-cent stamps are in a dozen. Now it has turned into a devastating tool in your mind-reading arsenal to be used to inflict bewilderment on innocent spectators.

Where did we go so wrong?

Because of interesting phenomena, freaky coincidences, and numerical oddities, it is possible to use mathematics to achieve "psychic" results. Most of these tricks, however, are basic and obvious. Except for the very young or the severely gullible, audiences will not be impressed by mathematical tricks. Yes, they work just fine; however, it is usually painfully obvious that evil mathematics is at work.

There is however, one glowing exception to this rule. It is called *What's Your Number?* and it is described in its entirety later in Chapter 11. The reason that I distinguish this well-crafted demonstration from others that use mathematics is because it camouflages the secret so cleverly. I have yet to see any spectator bring up the possibility that mathematics may be at work.

CODES WITH A PARTNER

While using a partner and a code system is challenging, it is also wickedly fun and immensely rewarding. For those of you who prefer working alone, you may decide to skip the routines that require the use of a partner. In my opinion, it would be a colossal mistake to omit this technique from your repertoire. Some of the most freakishly shocking demonstrations use partners and codes.

Are you worried that the audience will be able to detect that you are transmitting clues? Believe me, they won't. If you follow my tips, the codes will be hidden and will work *every time*. It is not as if I am going to have you broadcast clues like a third base coach. If the card selected is a four of hearts, I certainly won't suggest that you stomp your foot on the floor four times and place your hand over your heart.

When using a code system with a partner, there are three guidelines to follow:

• It must not appear as if clues are being transmitted.
• The signaler must use as few clues as possible.
• The code system must be relatively easy to understand.

The two demonstrations I present in this book that use codes meet each of these criteria. Upon first reading, these codes may appear complicated, but if you read through them carefully, you will see that they can be easily mastered.

All you will need is someone you trust, a large gymnasium, and six months of intense, nonstop training, and you will have learned a very small portion of a complex technique that will most likely never be of any use to you. Oh, wait a minute—that's square dancing.

What I meant to say was . . . All you will need is a few minutes of practice with a partner, and you will be able to dazzle, delight, and dumbfound the daylights out of your friends and family.

But, Is Using a Conspirator Cheating?

Using a conspirator is far different than working with a partner and is generally considered taboo, even among magicians. Whereas a partner transmits codes using cleverly hidden signals, a conspirator is nothing more than a plant in the audience, pretending to be a spectator. If this were acceptable, then anything would be possible. Here is why it is not fair:

You could have your spy "randomly" choose a card, "memorize" it, and then replace it back in the deck. Then all you would have to do is make up any card and the conspirator would say that you were correct. Since the audience never saw the card, they would think you just performed a miracle. It's foul. Except for large-scale performances where a conspirator is part of a big act, most magicians conisder using a conspirator to be cheating.

ONE AHEAD

This is mind reading at its finest. Perhaps the most brilliant mind-reading technique ever conceived, the one-ahead method can be used in a wide variety of psychic endeavors. The principle behind this system is knowing the identity of one card that will eventually be selected. This will allow you to perform startling feats of mentalism. The demonstration in Chapter 3 entitled *One Up* explains this technique in detail, and will surely become a standard part of your repertoire.

It's All in the Presentation

Brilliant tricks and flawless execution are only part of the formula for mind-reading success. If your goal is to deliver memorable performances, you will have to inject enthusiasm, showmanship, and style into each demonstration.

It is the act of selling it to the crowd through witty banter, entertaining stories, and tales of mystical powers and impossible feats of mentalism. As you read each chapter, be on the lookout for helpful hints on how to incorporate humor and mood into your performances.

Banter

Why settle for simply announcing the secret card to the audience when you can lead up to it by concocting a crazy story about a genie that granted you mystical powers when you were very young. Some people were blessed with natural athletic ability, others with superior intellect. You can explain that in place of these talents, you were given a power far greater . . . the ability to read minds. Who needs to be smart when you can just steal the answer from someone else's head?

Acting Stupid

Do you want to add an element of shock to your performances? Then make it seem as if you do not have a clue what you are doing. By second-guessing yourself and pretending to be inept, you will be setting up your skeptical audience for the surprise of their cozy, sheltered lives. Of course, acting like an idiot may come a little easier to some of us than others.

Some of these demonstrations allow you to add to the impact by pretending to be just as surprised as your audience at the outcome. You can add a touch of mystery by making it seem as if you really do not understand how the trick works.

Shuffling

Audiences are much more secure if they are allowed to inspect, handle, and mix the cards. They feel safe that no trickery can take place; no funny business can be conducted because the deck has been shuffled. It is as if the "deck demons" have been exorcized by this holy shuffling ritual.

Let them think that. Let these soon-to-be-shaken-from-their-world observers feel safe with their shuffling and reshuffling. In most cases, their obsessive mixing will have no bearing on the outcome. So, except where noted, feel free to encourage the audience to shuffle and reshuffle the cards until their fingers blister. The more secure they are that the deck is random, the more dumbfounded they will be when you conclude the demonstration. You can ask, "Are you sure the cards are mixed thoroughly? Maybe you would like to cut the deck a few times to be certain."

A word of caution: Since, in most cases, you *will* be doing some funny business with the cards, it is a good idea to shuffle the deck as soon as the demonstration is over. This way the evidence is spoiled and no one could accuse you of dirty dealing.

Top Secret

As difficult as it may be, you must not succumb to the pressure of your audience to reveal your secrets. Will they beg and plead to learn the solution to these demonstrations? Oh, yes. But you must not let them get to you.

This is important for two reasons: First and foremost, the impact of the demonstrations will be *significantly* reduced once your audience learns the secret. You will see how quickly their expressions transform from stupefied awe to disappointment. The second reason you do not want to reveal your well-practiced secrets is because you may want to perform some of these demonstrations for the same audience sometime in the future. Once the answer is known, you will have to remove that trick from your repertoire.

Warm-Up

Want to learn a fun mind reading experiment that you can use before you begin your routine? Select a volunteer from the audience and have her face the crowd. Blindfold her while someone else selects a card from the deck and shows it to the spectators.

Now everyone in the audience knows the card except for the blindfolded volunteer.

Announce to the audience that everyone has mind-reading ability to some extent, and you intend to prove it with this demonstration. Stand behind the volunteer and ask her to concentrate on the card. Within a few seconds, she is able to correctly identify the selected card.

How? Because you traced the card on her back with your finger! In most cases, this spectator will quickly figure out what you are doing and will be willing to play along. Everyone likes to be part of the act.

Rating System

I realize that you are very busy and don't have a lot of time to sift through every demonstration in this book, so I made it easy for you. Are you looking for a quick and easy trick to perform for a few friends? Or perhaps you need a spectacular, large-scale demonstration to impress a larger group. Check the rating system at the beginning of each chapter, and you will see which demo is right for you.

And how did I come up with these ratings, you wonder? Well, it is not as if I arbitrarily assigned random ratings without any forethought or basis of fact. Oh no. I had every demonstration rigorously tested at the International Center for Mind Reading and Handwriting Analysis in Helsinki, Finland (it's so cold there, brrrr).

Each was carefully scrutinized in the laboratory by a team of top-flight psychics and recently retired cheese salesmen. After their extensive analysis, it was then (and only then), that I sat down at my desk and arbitrarily assigned random ratings.

DIFFICULTY LEVEL: ✦✦✦✦✦

Some exhibitions are easy to execute and need little or no preparation. Others require extensive practice and rehearsal. It is generally a good strategy to begin with a few simple tricks before progressing to the more complex and impressive demonstrations. The higher the rating, the more difficult the demonstration will be to perform. Don't let this scare you! Follow the instructions and you will be an expert in no time.

IMPACT: ✳✳✳✳✳

In most cases, the impact and difficulty ratings are closely related. Like anything else in life, the more worthwhile endeavors require greater skill and have higher degrees of risk associated with them. By following the suggestions in the section with the gray bar along the edge entitled *Tips & Techniques* for each demonstration, you will achieve astonishing results with minimal danger of getting caught. Demos with impact ratings of two or three will generate moderate amazement; whereas ratings of four or five indicate mind-blowing showstoppers.

TECHNIQUE

The method used in each demonstration is stated in this section in the event you prefer one technique over another. To maximize the effectiveness of your routine, it is wise to learn a variety of methods to keep your audience guessing and entertained.

PREPARATION

The preparation required for the following demonstrations ranges from a simple presetting of a few cards to the memorization of names and addresses in the telephone book (believe it or not!). Is the extraordinary payoff worth the additional effort? Only you can decide. This section will indicate what type of preparation is needed.

One Up

3

DIFFICULTY LEVEL: ✦✦✦✦✦
IMPACT: ✳✳✳✳✳
TECHNIQUE: ONE AHEAD
PREPARATION: NONE

Overview

As described on page 12, the one-ahead principle is an innovative and powerful technique that is practically undetectable. All that is required for this demonstration is a deck of cards, a pencil, a sheet of paper, and a group of smug people who think mind reading is nothing more than a scam.

The Premise

To prove to the unbelieving audience that psychic powers do indeed exist, the mind reader proposes to conduct an experiment. He asks a spectator to make several piles of cards facedown on a table. Another member of the audience is then asked to select a pile, remove the top card, and concentrate on it. By using his "mystical powers," the mind reader will correctly identify the selected card. This process is repeated several times as the shell-shocked audience watches in awe.

How, you ask? Read on, and see how easy it is to read minds . . .

The Solution

It is the one-ahead principle that deserves the thanks for this little miracle. When you see how it works, you will want to try it immediately. By knowing the identity of one of the cards before the demonstration begins, you will be able to predict all cards chosen by *staying one ahead of the audience.*

17

Ah, but how will you know the identity of one of the cards ahead of time when the cards were mixed and separated into piles? Easy! After the audience shuffles the deck, you take the cards and perform one last shuffle. By slowing the shuffle down at the end, you will be able to catch a glimpse of the top card in the deck. This is the only card you have to remember. For the purpose of this explanation, let's assume that the top card is a **two of clubs.**

As stated in the premise, you will ask a spectator to create a series of piles. Make it understood that these piles should be created from the bottom of the deck and not the top. The easiest way to

accomplish this is by placing the deck on the table (facedown) and picking it up, leaving a few cards behind. You can demonstrate this simple technique on the first two piles, and then ask a spectator to continue with the rest of the deck. The spectator can make as many piles as he likes, but they all must be made the same way—from the bottom of the deck.

Remember that the top card on the very last pile will be the card that you saw during your sneaky shuffle—the two of clubs.

So now you have several piles of cards in front of you on the table. As explained earlier, you ask a spectator to point to a pile, pick up the top card, and concentrate on it. Using your phony psychic powers, you read the spectator's thoughts and write down your prediction on a piece of paper.

Since you don't really have psychic powers, how will you know what to write down? Well, you won't know, but it doesn't matter. Whatever card is selected, you jot down the two of clubs, *making sure no one sees the prediction.*

You then ask the spectator to reveal the card he selected. He will think that it is perfectly fine to reveal the card now, since you already wrote your prediction on the paper. Let's assume that this card was the **queen of diamonds**. You nod your head smugly as if your prediction was correct. Another spectator is asked to point to a different pile, pick up the top card, and concentrate on it. Once again, use your powers to read the spectator's mind. You then write down your prediction of this new card on the same piece of paper. What will you write this time? *The card that the first spectator selected—the queen of diamonds.*

As before, the second spectator is then asked to reveal the card. Let's say that this card is a **six of spades**. Another spectator then selects the top card off of a different pile. This time, you write down the previously-selected card—the six of spades. The spectator then reveals that it was an **eight of clubs**. Can you see where this is going? Take a look at this chart to see what has happened thus far:

Cards selected by spectators	Cards written on paper
1. Queen of diamonds	1. Two of clubs
2. Six of spades	2. Queen of diamonds
3. Eight of clubs	3. Six of spades

You are always "one ahead" of the audience. Remember, the two of clubs is still on top of one of the piles. You are just waiting for someone to select that card, and you can end the demonstration with a dramatic finish. And, let's face it—the two of clubs will eventually be selected since piles cannot be selected twice.

On average, there will be six to eight piles of cards on the table. It is just a matter of time before someone chooses the pile with the two of clubs on top.

Let's assume that the next card chosen is the two of clubs. All you have to do is write down the previous card selected (in this case, the eight of clubs), and then your list matches the cards chosen. The only step that remains is to show the list to your skeptical audience.

You now know all you need to perform this demonstration successfully. See *Tips & Techniques* on the next page for insider secrets and fun performance suggestions.

19

Tips & Techniques

This is such a great technique. Once you sneak a peak at the top card, there are no moves, tricks, or shenanigans to execute. With some acting and showmanship, *One Up* will work flawlessly every time.

Let's discuss a few points that may help you improve the performance and make it extremely difficult for the audience to catch on.

As you read in the premise, the spectator is free to choose the number of piles and how many cards will be in each pile. This is important because it proves to the audience that the piles are completely random. It is even more impressive when you name the cards on top of each pile since you had nothing to do with creating the piles.

The demonstration will lose impact, however, if your volunteer tries to make 40 piles out of the deck. Ideally, you would like to see six to eight piles, but a few more will not influence the final result. If you see that the spectator is making ridiculously small piles, tell her to limit the number to ten. You started the process by making the first two piles, so chances are they will follow your lead and keep the sizes of the piles relatively the same.

When the entire deck has been made into piles, I recommend that you perform one final step before predicting the cards. Turn around and invite the audience to mix up the order of the piles while you are not looking. I don't mean to mix up the cards in the piles; I mean the order (put the third pile where the first pile was, etc.).

The reason I suggest this is because when the demonstration is over, it might occur to someone that you did sneak a peak at the top card when you shuffled the deck. (Can you believe how paranoid some people can be?) Rearranging the piles will steer them away from that suspicion.

If the piles are rearranged, you will no longer know which pile contains the two of clubs, but it doesn't matter. All you need to know is that this card is on top of one of the piles. It makes no difference which one. They will get to it sooner or later.

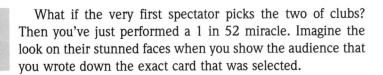 What if the very first spectator picks the two of clubs? Then you've just performed a 1 in 52 miracle. Imagine the look on their stunned faces when you show the audience that you wrote down the exact card that was selected.

The Shuffle

The key to this demonstration is sneaking a peek at the top card when you shuffle the deck at the beginning of the demonstration. This is actually a simple move and can be accomplished perfectly after only a few practice attempts.

If you do not like the idea of peeking at the top card, here is an alternate suggestion: After a spectator has thoroughly shuffled the cards, you can tell the audience that this demonstration will be successful only if you make sure there are no jokers in the deck. You then have a reason to pick up the cards and look through them quickly, taking note of the top card. Once you determine there are no jokers, place the cards on the table and begin the demonstration.

The List

Here is a snag: If you write down the two of clubs first, won't it seem odd? I mean, the two of clubs was selected *last,* so why would it be written *first?* Won't that seem a bit askew to an observant audience? Of course it will. Here's how to overcome that challenge:

To ensure that the two of clubs is the last card written on your list, write it approximately two inches from the top. The *second* prediction should be written at the very top of the paper. Each subsequent prediction will then be written below this card, working downward on the paper, making sure that the two of clubs remains at the bottom of the list. This will make it seem that you did write the cards in the order they were selected.

If you prefer, you can write each prediction on a separate piece of paper, fold it up, and place it on the table. When you have completed the predictions, you can shuffle the papers to mix up the order and give them to a spectator to read to the audience.

21

Behind the Back

DIFFICULTY LEVEL: ✦✦✦✦✦
IMPACT: ✳✳✳✳✳
TECHNIQUE: ONE AHEAD
PREPARATION: NONE

Overview

Rarely will you find a mind-reading demonstration that is easier to perform than *Behind the Back*. This is another feat that uses the one-ahead principle as its primary method. There is no guesswork and the trick is 99% foolproof.

The Premise

In this demonstration, the mind reader will accurately predict upcoming cards in an ordinary deck.

Step 1: The mind reader asks a spectator to shuffle a deck of cards. When the audience is satisfied that the cards have been thoroughly mixed, the deck is handed back to the mind reader. In plain view of everyone, the mind reader takes the cards and brings them behind his back, holding them with both hands.

Step 2: The mind reader explains that he will bring the cards from behind his back and hold up the deck so that only the audience can see the front card. He demonstrates this procedure by holding the deck in front of him at arm's length. In this manner, he is unable to see the front card. The audience, however, can see it clearly.

Step 3: Once this method has been demonstrated, the mind reader puts the deck behind his back again and shuffles a little to bring a new card to the front of the deck. He then holds the deck in front of him as before and *tells the audience the identity of the front card.* He does this, presumably, without ever having seen the card.

Solution

Some of the best solutions are the simplest. As stated in step one, you will bring the cards behind your back, hidden from the audience. With one hand, grab a stack of 20 cards or so and *flip them over.* You heard me, just flip them right over. This way, *cards are faceup on the top and the bottom of the deck.* Does this make sense? No matter which way you look at the deck, cards will be faceup.

Why is this important? Well, when you hold your arm out to show the deck to the audience, they will be looking at the face of a card. Since they see the face of the card, they will assume that you are looking at the back of a card. But this isn't the case! You will actually be looking directly at the face of a card; granted, not the same card that they see, but it does not matter.

The card you are looking at will be the very next card the audience will see. Remember, at this point, you haven't actually started the process yet; you are supposedly holding your arm out to show the audience how the demonstration will be conducted. The real reason you are doing this, however, is to get a glimpse of the first card facing you. For the sake of this explanation, let's assume that the card you see is an **eight of diamonds**.

Once you see the identity of this card, tell the audience it is now time to begin the demonstration. You then bring the cards behind your back, holding them with both hands.

All you have to do is take the eight of diamonds and move it to the opposite end of the deck, facing out. This way, when you bring your arm forward again, the audience will be staring directly at this card. Ask the spectators to concentrate on the card they see. After flexing your mind reading muscles and making strenuous faces, you correctly identify the eight of diamonds.

By the way, while you are naming the card, you are also looking at the next card that is facing you. Let's assume that card is a **queen of clubs**. This allows you to repeat this miracle over and over. Bring the deck behind your back again, move the queen to the front, and repeat the process. If you like, you can continue naming cards until all of the cards facing you have been used.

Tips & Techniques

The best part of this demonstration is that you are executing the move out of sight of the audience. When you move your hands behind your back and flip a card over, the audience will assume that you are simply shuffling the deck. If you practice this maneuver, you will learn to flip the cards quickly and unnoticeably.

Behind the Back allows you to have some fun with isolated members of the audience. This can be accomplished by allowing several of the observers to stand behind you during the performance. By doing this, you are letting a small group of people in on the secret. If you position these observers there before the demonstration, they will be aware that you are intentionally letting them see the solution, and will generally go along with the setup.

If you try this variation, you can also include these onlookers standing behind you in the performance. After you have identified several cards correctly, you can pretend you are having a hard time with the next card and ask a spectator behind you for assistance. Remember: they can see everything behind you, so they know the identity of each card you hold up to the audience. You can ask this spectator if he can "feel" or "read" the color of the card, then the suit, and eventually the card itself.

I use this demonstration as a warm-up to the more challenging and impressive feats described later in the book. If I let them in on this secret, I then tell them that this was just a gimmick; the "real" acts of mind reading are yet to come.

5

Under the Table

DIFFICULTY LEVEL: ✦✦✦✦✦
IMPACT: ✸✸✸✸✸
TECHNIQUE: FALSE ASSUMPTION/SLEIGHT OF HAND
PREPARATION: NONE

Overview

Under the Table is a great icebreaker and works especially well for small groups. All you need is an ordinary deck of cards and a table to prove your superhuman talents. This demonstration ranks among the more unusual as it all takes place under a table!

The Premise

The mind reader sits across a table from an observer.

Step 1: The mind reader asks his observer to inspect an ordinary deck of cards. She is invited to look at them, both front and back, and to count the cards to make sure there are indeed 52 in the deck. Once this is confirmed, the deck is handed back to the mind reader.

    The mind reader then lowers his hands underneath the table, holding the deck of cards. He asks the observer to place her hands under the table and take the cards. The observer will explore until she feels the deck. She then takes the cards from the mind reader as instructed.

Step 2: The observer is asked to shuffle the deck thoroughly, while keeping her hands under the table. She is not permitted to look under the table at the cards. Once she is satisfied that the deck has been thoroughly mixed, she hands the cards back to the mind reader, still keeping the cards under the table.

Step 3: The mind reader fans the deck out under the table, and asks the observer to pick out a card, look at it, and then reach back under the table to replace the card in the deck. The observer then takes the deck, mixes the cards thoroughly (keeping them under the table), and then hands them back to the mind reader.

Step 4: The mind reader looks through the deck and picks out the card that the observer selected.

Solution

The secret behind this gem is a basic sleight of hand maneuver. Although it is plausible that astute spectators can solve this demo, it is impossible for them to actually see you executing the move. This is because it takes place under the table.

After the observer selects a card, she pulls it out from under the table to look at it. While she is doing this, *you simply turn the deck upside down.* It's that easy! Instead of all of the cards facing down, they will now be facing up. When the observer reaches back under the table to replace the card back into the deck, she will automatically place the card *facedown.*

26

And why wouldn't she? Since she cannot see the deck, she will assume that the cards are all facedown. And she has absolutely no reason to think otherwise. After all, the cards were facing down when she first saw the deck, and the card she selected was facedown when she drew it from the pack. Unless she is very suspicious or extremely clever, she will have no clue that the deck has been flipped over.

After she replaces the card in the deck, it will be crystal clear which card was selected—the only one that is facedown.

Once the card has been put back into the deck, the observer can shuffle or cut the deck—repeatedly if she likes, since doing so will not change the way the cards are facing. As long as she is not permitted to look at the cards while she is shuffling, she will never catch on. When the observer hands the deck back to you under the table, glance down at the cards (keeping them out of sight of the spectators) until you find the one that is facedown.

Tips & Techniques

What a bizarre and fun demonstration to perform. It works even better when there are several people seated in a circle, and everyone has their hands under the table. The deck can be passed from person to person—under the table—to be shuffled.

While the observers are mixing the cards under the table, you can begin your explanation of the powers bestowed upon you at your birth by a mystical wizard who lives atop a mountain deep in the heart of Tibet. You were given two talents: mind reading and the ability to come very close to guessing the exact time without a clock in sight. It is the mind-reading talent that you would like to demonstrate; however you would be happy to take a stab at the correct time when the feat is over.

By this point, the deck should be fully shuffled and back in your hands to continue the demonstration. If you are performing *Under the Table* for a group of people, make sure that the observer who selects the card shows it to all spectators.

Be careful not to mishandle the cards. Since neither you nor your spectators will be looking at the deck while shuffling, cutting, selecting, and passing the cards, there is a tendency for some cards to fall to the ground. This makes for a very sloppy presentation and greatly diminishes the impact of the final result. Caution the spectators to handle the cards with care and not to drop any.

A Great Finish!

There is a great way of presenting the climax of this demonstration to increase its overall impact. Once you identify the selected card, secretly move it to approximately the eighth position from the top of the deck, and then place the cards on the table (all cards should be facing down at this point).

After some general banter about the importance of everyone concentrating on the card that was selected, you pick up the deck and begin to turn over the cards, one at a time. When you reach the card the spectator chose, *don't say or do anything!* Just keep turning cards over one by one until another seven or eight have passed.

Then grab hold of the next card, as if you are about to turn it over, and say, "Now, I am sure that the very next card I turn over will be the card you selected." And if you are the gambling type, you can say, "How much do you want to bet that the next card I turn over is the one you selected?"

What's great about this little deception is that the observer already saw his card turned over and placed on the table. How confident he must feel! He must be thinking that there is no possible way the next card could be his, since he can see it already sitting on the table! He sees you poised to turn over another card, and he knows that he has you beat! It would not be unusual for him to wager huge sums of money that the very next card you turn over *will not be* the card he selected.

Imagine his surprise when he sees you put the deck down and then reach over to the discarded pile and pick out his card. Once you pick it up, show the card to your observer, and then turn it over on the table. The very next card you turned over was indeed the card he had originally selected.

6

The Envelope, Please

DIFFICULTY LEVEL: ✦✦✦✦✦
IMPACT: ✸✸✸✸✸
TECHNIQUE: SLEIGHT OF HAND
PREPARATION: MINIMAL

Overview

This remarkably easy demonstration packs a powerful punch. It begins with an unfathomable prediction and ends with a baffling display of mental telepathy.

The Premise

The mind reader asks an observer to shuffle the cards thoroughly, explaining that the only way this demonstration will work properly is if the cards are completely mixed and random. After a few shuffles, she asks the observer if the cards are indeed shuffled to his satisfaction. Once this is confirmed, the mind reader asks the observer if he wants to cut the deck—it is entirely up to him.

Whether the observer decides to cut the deck or not is inconsequential. Once he assures the mind reader that he is 100% confident that the cards are mixed and random, the mind reader casually places a sealed envelope on top of the deck.

The mind reader then explains to the audience that she made a prediction, wrote it on a piece of paper, and sealed it inside the envelope. She states that the prediction she wrote will match the top card on the deck.

Once the audience expresses their disbelief, she asks another observer to pick up the envelope, open it, and remove the piece of paper. This observer is then asked to announce the card written on the paper. Once this is done, the mind reader asks another observer to turn over the top card.

And does the prediction match the card? Of course it does, or else this would be quite a lame demonstration. But how is it done, you ask? Read on . . .

Solution

Before your performance, write the name of a card on a piece of paper and seal it in an envelope. For the sake of this explanation, let's assume that your prediction is the **five of clubs**. Once you have written your prediction, place it in an envelope, and seal it. Then look through the deck and remove the five of clubs.

Hold the five of clubs *underneath* the envelope, facedown. Now you are ready to begin the demonstration. After the observer shuffles the deck and puts it back on the table, all you have to do is place the envelope on top of the deck. Since the five of clubs is underneath the envelope, it will now be the top card in the deck. Sneaky!*

Tips & Techniques

I love how the audience is lulled into a false sense of security. After all, the deck was shuffled completely, and you never had a chance to handle it. How could you possibly have known what the top card was? The icing on the cake is that you asked the observer whether he wanted to cut the deck after it had been shuffled.

You can point all this out to the audience when the demonstration is over. Tell them that you never came near the deck and that the observer had every opportunity to mix up the cards. They will be thinking: "Ah, if only he had/had not decided to cut those cards! The demonstration never would have worked." Mention that you took all of that into account before making a prediction. You knew whether or not the observer would cut the deck. That's why you predicted the five of clubs. Had he cut the deck, you would have predicted a different card.

* Made you look

The only technical point you should keep in mind is that the card underneath the envelope must be positioned in the same direction as the rest of the deck. Place the card directly on top of the deck as if it had been there all along. You will raise suspicion if the card is angled badly.

When you lay the envelope on the deck, do so in one smooth motion. Do not attempt to straighten it. It should appear as if you don't care where you placed the envelope; it randomly landed on top of the deck.

 ## *A Fun Tip!*

Instead of sealing the prediction before you begin the demonstration, wait until after the deck is shuffled to do so. This way, you can use your "special techniques" to identify the top card. It's hysterical! Here are two options:

• Once the cards are shuffled, walk over to the deck and—without touching it—examine it closely. Look at it intently, sniff it, listen to it, pretend to have a conversation with it (laugh at its jokes, argue with it, nod understandingly). If you really feel like hamming it up, relay to the audience the story that the deck just told you.

31

Now that the deck has "told" you what its top card is, write a prediction on a piece of paper, fold it up, place it in an envelope, and then seal the envelope. Continue with the demonstration as described above.

• If you prefer, you can use a slight variation. Once the deck has been thoroughly shuffled, place an empty envelope on top. Underneath the envelope, of course, will be the five of clubs. At this point, you explain the purpose of the demonstration to the audience. You tell them that you want someone to lift up the top card and pass it around, without letting you see it.

After the audience has seen the card, it is replaced on top of the deck. Now you can try your amusing little mind reading stunts. Either "listen" to the deck for clues, or maybe use your mystical talents to read the minds of the audience. This is a great opportunity to demonstrate to the spectators how you can understand their thoughts by studying their palms, or feeling the bumps on their heads, or just about any wacky antic you can imagine. Then write your prediction and seal it in the envelope.

The advantage of this version is that it becomes a little more difficult for the audience to discover the solution. Now they have to wonder whether perhaps you sneaked a peak at a card, or received clues from someone in the audience, or maybe, just maybe, you really did read their minds.

Seven Up

DIFFICULTY LEVEL: ✦✦✦✦✦
IMPACT: ✹✹✹✹✹ OR ✹✹✹✹✹
TECHNIQUE: FORCED CARD/PRESET DECK
PREPARATION: VERY LITTLE

Overview

Did you happen to catch a glimpse of the impact rating for this demonstration? There seems to be a bit of confusion. I know what you're thinking: "Is this a one-star trick or a four-star trick? Should I even bother learning the trick if it could be a flop? I wonder if there are any donuts left." (See how well I've gotten to know you?)

Well, here's the deal: When *Seven Up* works, it's magical; when it doesn't, it's a flop. Normally, I wouldn't teach you a demonstration where there is a more than a slight chance that you could be discovered, but this one is worth making an exception.

Although *Seven-Up* is flawless most of the time, there are instances when—due to circumstances beyond your control—you may not be able to influence the outcome. I will, however, teach you methods to minimize the risk of being discovered and run out of town by an angry mob.

Seven Up is a standard demonstration in my repertoire; but I still keep my fingers crossed when I perform it!

The Premise

The mind reader asks several members of the audience to help select a card through a *process of elimination*. When a spectator narrows the deck down to a single card, the mind reader produces that very card from the top of the deck (or the bottom or perhaps from his pocket!).

The Setup

Before performing *Seven Up,* you must pre-arrange the deck as follows:
- Seven of spades on top of the deck
- Seven of clubs on the bottom of the deck
- Seven of diamonds in the middle of the deck *turned over* (it will be the only card facing up)
- Seven of hearts in your shirt pocket

You then place the deck face-down (not spread) on a table. You can even put the deck back in the case and leave it on the table before you perform the demonstration.

Solution

The secret to this demonstration uses a basic technique to force a card on the audience. The following explanation describes a worst-case scenario. Rarely will the audience's responses be exactly opposite what you want them to be. Life is just not that cruel. But in case you run into a bit of bad luck, this description will show you how the demonstration would play out. More likely scenarios will be discussed in *Tips & Techniques*.

Begin this demonstration by announcing to your audience that you would like to perform an experiment in "elimination." You then say to a spectator, "Eliminating the picture cards, please select either odd or even cards."

If the spectator chooses even cards, you say, "So we eliminate the even cards. That leaves us with only the odd cards." This narrows the deck to just the ones (aces), threes, fives, sevens, and nines. You then choose another spectator and say, "Eliminating the ace, please select an odd card." Now only the threes, fives, sevens, and nines remain.

If the spectator says anything other than seven—let's assume a three—you say, "So we eliminate the three." You then find another spectator and say, "That leaves us with 5, 7, and 9. Eliminating the 5 please select a card."

Since the only two cards that remain are the 7 and 9, there is a 50% chance that the spectator will choose a 7 and put you out of your misery. But if she selects 9, you say, "Eliminating the 9, we are left with a 7." You then select someone from the audience and say, "Can you please name a suit?"

Since you pre-arranged the cards, whatever suit is selected, you are able to provide the appropriate card from the deck or from your pocket.

Tips & Techniques

See what I mean? Won't it be embarrassingly obvious to the audience that you forced them to pick a seven? The answer, more often than not, is no! Let me show you why.

The scenario that I described above is highly unlikely because each time the audience made the wrong choice. You wanted them to select odd cards, they chose even; you wanted them to pick the seven, they avoided the seven like a . . . like a . . . well, fill in your own simile here. The point is that they weren't giving you any help at all.

It is likelier that their responses will be more favorable. The goal, obviously, is to have the audience select a seven early in the demonstration. Let's look at other possible scenarios.

When you ask a spectator to select odd or even cards, you have a 50% chance of her choosing odd. If this is the case, you proceed directly into the rest of the demo. If even is selected, you simply announce that even has been eliminated. After all, you did mention at the beginning of the demonstration that this was an exercise in elimination. The audience generally does not have a problem with that—at this point.

Once the odd or even cards have been selected, you have a 25% chance of getting the seven right off the bat. Why? Because the odd cards are the one (ace), three, five, seven, and nine. After you "eliminate" the ace, there are only four left. The reason that I chose seven as the magic card is because it seems to be the most common number picked.

Can you imagine the audience's reaction if the very first card chosen is a seven? You will immediately be hoisted upon their shoulders and proclaimed the greatest psychic to walk the earth. And this will happen *at least* 25% of the time. Unfortunately, this is a best-case scenario, and usually you have to work a little harder. But when it does occur, play it up with as much hokey showmanship as possible, because it will create a stunning reaction.

So let's assume that the first card chosen was a three. You eliminate it from the pool, and narrow it down even further. At this point, the only cards left are the five, seven, and nine. You then go on to the final step by saying, "Now, eliminating the five, that leaves us with a seven or nine."

Now you have a 50% chance of the next spectator selecting the seven. Actually, it works out fine if she chooses the nine, since you can simply eliminate it and end up with the seven after all.

It is important not to make it apparent that you are steering the audience toward a particular card. Actually, the trick makes perfect sense if you *consistently eliminate* the audience's selection all the way down to the seven, like this:

Remaining Choices	Audience Selection	Outcome
Odd or even ➞	Even ➞	Even is eliminated
3, 5, 7, or 9 ➞	Three ➞	Three is eliminated
7 or 9 ➞	Nine ➞	Nine is eliminated

Leaving seven. But what happens if you start in the path of elimination, and then suddenly someone chooses a seven. You certainly won't eliminate the seven, will you? Could you possibly justify why all of a sudden you arbitrarily stopped eliminating? Won't it seem obvious that you eliminate only when the audience chooses what you don't want them to?

It's a risk. So here is how you can minimize the chance of someone catching on:
• If the audience chooses odd cards and then chooses a seven, there is no need to eliminate anything; continue with the

demonstration. But didn't you mention at the beginning that this was an exercise in elimination? What if someone asks what that was all about? You simply say that you eliminated the picture cards (which you did); that was what you meant. They will not question you further.

• If the audience chooses even cards, you eliminate them. Remember, even though you now have a 25% chance of the seven being selected, it seems to be chosen more frequently than any other card. This means there is a good chance the demo could end here.

If the spectator does not choose seven, you need an escape plan. You say, "We now need to narrow it down further. Eliminating the ace, please select one of the remaining numbers." By mentioning that you are narrowing it down, you introduce the notion that you are simply limiting the field, and not selecting a final number.

So, if a spectator chooses something other than the seven, it will seem perfectly natural that you eliminate it. If a spectator chooses the seven, then you have still "narrowed it down" to a seven, because the suit still needs to be selected.

• Potential danger arises during the next part. Let's say that a three was chosen, leaving you with the five, seven, and nine. You will eliminate the five (or nine, it is up to you) leaving only two choices.

If a seven is not chosen, the trick will seem perfectly natural. This is because during each step of the demonstration, you eliminated whatever the audience chose. It makes sense that you will eliminate the five and leave the seven, since you have been eliminating all along.

But! What if the seven is now chosen? Won't it look awfully suspicious that you keep the seven instead of eliminating it? Yes; it will look very suspicious. So much so that if you do not prepare for this possibility, you will be discovered, disgraced, and deported. Here is how to combat that possibility:

Before asking an audience member to choose between the final two cards, you need to present a dramatic finish. Play it up as much as you can—silence the audience, ask for

37

a drum roll, make everyone chant something in unison—whatever you can do to indicate that a grand finale is coming. You can even say, "We have narrowed it down to just two cards. Now it is the time to make the final selection. Are you ready to choose the final card?"

This way, if the spectator selects seven, you can continue with excitement as if this is where you intended to end the demonstration. After all, you did just say that the spectator was about to choose the "final card." If you play it right, the audience will be swept away with the excitement, and you can continue on to select a suit.

If, however, the spectator selects the nine instead, you can still proceed to a dramatic finish. With great enthusiasm, you can say, "So, eliminating the nine, leaves us with . . . ?" When the audience answers seven, you proceed to the suits.

• In this last scenario, if an audience member accuses you of forcing the seven through selective elimination, you can prove that you did no such thing, since you eliminated every choice the audience made.

Selecting a Suit

You can have the audience select a suit either by direct choice or by elimination. Keep in mind that the deck is pre-arranged. The sevens have been strategically placed to allow each suit to generate tremendous impact. It doesn't matter which suit is selected.

• If you have been eliminating the spectators' choices for most of the trick, continue with elimination. But this time, stress to the audience that you will be eliminating all suits until only one remains.

• Make sure the audience understands fully that each suit *will be* eliminated. This way the rules have been established and no one can accuse you of waiting until you heard the suit that you wanted.

• If you have not been eliminating the spectators' choices, then ask directly for a suit. Tell the audience that whatever suit is selected will be the final answer. If you decide upon this option, make sure that you emphasize that there will be *no elimination whatsoever* when selecting the suit. This way you cannot be accused of eliminating only when it benefits you.

Which suit should you hope is selected? It really doesn't matter. Remember:

- Seven of spaces on top of deck
- Seven of clubs on bottom of deck
- Seven of diamonds in the middle of the deck, but faceup (all other cards are facedown)
- Seven of hearts in your pocket

Strong Finish

This is where you can have the most fun. Feel free to take your time and ham it up as much as you want. At this point, the risk is over, the card has been selected, and there is no possible way the demonstration can fail. You can breathe a sigh of relief and take your time.

- If the seven of spades has been chosen, ask a spectator to remove the deck from the case and place it on the table. Ask another spectator to remove the top card and show it to the audience.
- If it is the seven of clubs, simply ask the spectator to hold the deck up to the audience and show the bottom card.
- If the seven of diamonds is chosen (my favorite), ask the spectator to fan out the cards. The audience will immediately notice that the only card facing up is the seven of diamonds.
- If the seven of hearts is chosen, take the card out of your shirt pocket and show it to the audience, mentioning that the seven of hearts was kept safely by your own heart.

Gasps, mouths agape, shrieks, and cries of *"Oh my God, how did you DO that?"* will fill the room. There's only one last task to perform before ending the demonstration. Casually take the deck and give it a quick shuffle. If the seven of diamonds was not selected, make sure that you locate it and turn it back over. This is because within a few seconds, the audience will start to wonder how the trick was performed, and will invariably ask to inspect the deck. If you innocently shuffle it once before placing it back on the table, they will not see the other sevens in obvious places.

39

As a final note, you should realize that, mathematically, you have a much better than 50-50 chance the audience will make favorable selections. This means that in most cases, *Seven Up* will go off without a hitch. On occasion, the audience will not answer favorably and you will need to use some of the techniques discussed in this chapter to save the demonstration. In my opinion, the likely successful payoff of this feat far outweighs the risks of being discovered.

8

How Did I Do That?

DIFFICULTY LEVEL: ✦✦✦✦✦
IMPACT: ✳✳✳✳✳
TECHNIQUE: PRESET DECK OR FALSE ASSUMPTION (TWO VERSIONS)
PREPARATION: SOME

Overview

Once you learn this demonstration, it will quickly become a favorite in your repertoire. What makes it so spectacular is that it is the spectators who are performing the mind reading!

I am going to present two versions of this feat. The first requires a preset deck, whereas the second version can use any ordinary deck of cards.

The Premise

In this demonstration, two spectators will use their psychic ability to correctly guess the color of every card in the deck. It will play out as follows:

Step 1: The mind reader announces that for the next exhibition, it will be the audience that uses their mind reading skills. To demonstrate this, he selects a spectator and asks her to place each card in one of two piles—the red cards on the left pile and the black cards on the right pile. The only stipulation is that the spectator cannot look at any of the cards before placing them in a pile.

"How am I supposed to know the color of the card without looking at it?" your bewildered spectator will surely ask. The mind reader tells her that if she concentrates, her inner voice will reveal whether the card is red or black.

41

Step 2: The mind reader then takes two red cards and two black cards from the deck. He places one red card faceup and one black card faceup, right next to each other on the table (he saves the other two cards for later). He tells the audience that these cards will be the markers for the two piles.

The mind reader hands the deck to the spectator and asks her to go through the pile one by one and **place the red cards facedown on the red pile and the black cards facedown on the black pile—without looking at the cards, of course.** This process continues until half the deck has been depleted.

Step 3: At this point, there will be two facedown piles on the table, one is presumably the red cards (on the left) and the other is the black cards (on the right). **The mind reader then says it is time to make a switch.**

Remember those two cards that the mind reader was saving in Step Two (one black and one red)? **He places the black card faceup on the red pile, and the red card faceup on the black pile** (see diagram).

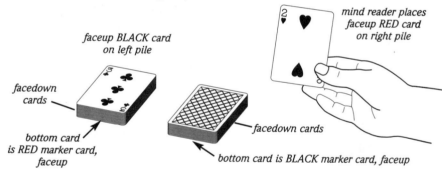

mind reader places
faceup RED card
on right pile

*faceup BLACK card
on left pile*

*facedown
cards*

*bottom card
is RED marker card,
faceup*

facedown cards

bottom card is BLACK marker card, faceup

Step 4: There is no Step Four.

Step 5: So, here we go: The pile on the left has a red card faceup on the bottom, a bunch of cards piled on it facedown, and now a black card facing up on top. The pile on the right is exactly reversed (a black card on the bottom, a bunch of cards piled on it facedown, and now a red card facing up on top).

The second spectator is asked to place the black cards on the pile on the left (facedown) and the red cards on the pile on the right (facedown), one at a time—still without peeking. This continues until the entire deck is finished.

Step 6: The mind reader then turns over the piles to reveal that the spectators guessed the color of every card correctly! Is this insane? Of course it is! How is this possible?

Solution

Here's the solution in a nutshell:

Before you begin the demonstration, you will preset the deck with all the red cards on top and the black cards on the bottom. Knowing this, let's review the demonstration.

The first spectator guesses the color of the cards and places them on the appropriate piles facedown. After half the deck has been guessed, there will be two piles of cards—some on the red pile (left side) and some on the black pile (right side). The funny thing is that all the cards are red!

When half the deck has been guessed, there will be only black cards left. The second spectator will continue guessing the cards until there are no more cards left. At this point, the cards will look as follows:

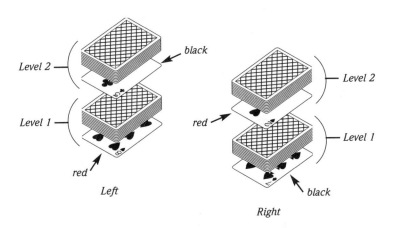

Since the deck has been preset, you know that all the cards facedown in Level 1 are red, and all the cards facedown in Level 2 are black. The challenge is for you to group the red cards in Level 1 together and the black cards in Level 2 together before you reveal them to the audience.

43

Easier said than done? Perhaps, but if you follow the suggestions in *Tips & Techniques* below, it will work perfectly every time.

Once the cards are grouped properly, you turn them over to reveal all black in one pile and all red in the other. Then stand by with smelling salts to revive your shocked and terrified audience.

Tips & Techniques

After you preset the deck, there will be 26 red cards on top and 26 black cards on the bottom. Since you removed two black cards and two red cards (to be used as pile markers), there will be only 24 red cards and 24 black cards. You will have to count the red cards as they are being placed in the piles so that you know when only black cards remain.

What this means to you is that when Spectator #1 is guessing card colors, *you must silently keep count and stop her after the 24th card has been placed.* This way, all the red cards will have been removed, leaving only 24 cards left—all black.

Okay, so let's see how this plays out: After Spectator #1 counts off 24 cards, you take the deck and give it to Spectator #2. Before he starts counting, remember to place the two cards you have saved on the appropriate piles as markers (red card on the black pile and black card on the red pile—faceup; see the diagram on page 42).

After Spectator #2 finishes placing the cards where he wants, it is time to execute the move. To make this demonstration perfect, you need to group the colors together and turn the four piles into just two. There are many ways to accomplish this; here is one suggestion:

Talk to the audience about probability and statistics (see below for hints). While you are talking, scoop up the four faceup cards that are left on the table and put them aside. Continue your banter as you nonchalantly pick up the two red piles and place them on top of one another facedown. Do the same with the black piles.

Since you separated the cards into these piles away from the markers, the audience will not remember which piles were red and which were black. All they know is that there are now two piles, one of which is supposedly red and one supposedly black. Also, they will be concentrating on your banter; certainly not on which pile is going on top of which. Besides, all you are doing is placing one pile on top of another. How could simply placing one pile on top of another pile miraculously turn all of them one color?

Yes, technically, it is a sleight of hand. But you are executing the move in plain view, right in front of them. The move is so blatant that you will get away with it every time.

Other Tips

- By performing the demonstration the way it was described above, you've just proven that your audience members are intuitive and have strong ESP. But you may decide that it is more fun to achieve the opposite effect. If you reversed the order in which you gathered the piles, you could arrange it so that the spectators are 100% wrong!
- Whether you let the audience be 100% right or 100% wrong, you could prolong the climax of the demonstration. Instead of having the spectator flip over all the cards at once, you can ask her to turn over only the top card, then the

next, then the next, etc. This will build suspense and have a much more lasting impression on the audience.

Imagine how the audience's reaction will build when the fourth, fifth, sixth, and seventh cards are all red. After revealing a dozen or so, you could then flip over the rest of the cards.

• Are you wondering how you will preset the cards when everyone is looking at you? I have a solution: Don't do it when people are looking at you. Obviously, you must have the deck ready before you even begin discussing the premise with the audience.

The first suggestion I have for you is to perform this demonstration after you have already performed several others. In fact, after you finish a trick, and the audience is wondering *how you did that,* it would be a good time to casually preset the deck. Once the cards are in order, do not immediately attempt to perform this demonstration; rather, place the cards on the table and let them sit for a moment.

After the conversation about your last feat of mind reading has subsided, you can slowly reach over and pick the deck up again to start the new demonstration. Since this is the same deck that you have been using in your other tricks, the audience will assume that it is already well shuffled.

And what if someone asks what you are doing? Brush it off, shuffle the cards, and try a different demonstration. Save this one for later.

A much simpler option would be for you to have a spare deck of cards. This deck must look completely identical to the original deck. After several demonstrations have been performed, casually replace the first deck with the second deck (already preset). This will eliminate any chance of getting caught setting up the deck.

• As a spectator places cards on the piles, you can stop him and ask if he is sure about a certain placement. Give him the opportunity to switch piles if he wants. As a humorous twist, after a spectator places a red card on the black pile, stop the demonstration, and pick up the card. Tell her she must have momentarily lost her concentration and made a mistake. Pick up the card, show it to the audience and then place it on the correct pile.

- If the spectator places the first card on the red pile, you can confidently turn it over to show the audience that it is correct, remarking that you think this is going to turn out quite well. If the first card is placed on the black pile, just continue with the demonstration as described.

- Are you wondering what happens if a wise guy in the audience places *all* the cards on the red pile (or black pile for that matter)? Wow, reader, I am very impressed! You really think of everything. Well, there is no need to panic; in fact, it could work out to your advantage.

    Once the 24 cards have been placed in the red pile, you tell him to stop, saying that that is about half the deck. This means that all the other cards must be black. Ask him to turn over the cards, revealing that they are indeed black. Certainly not as spectacular as planned, but it will work nonetheless.

Banter

As you are about to perform the sleight of hand maneuver, you should give the audience a lesson in probability and statistics. Not only will this talk be entertaining, but it will hide the fact that you are being sneaky.

The lesson is as follows: If you were to flip a coin, what are the chances that it will land on heads? The audience will generally say 50-50, which is exactly correct. You then ask the crowd that if the first flip was heads, what are the chances that heads would turn up on the second flip? Would the chances decrease since it landed on heads on the first flip? The answer to this question is no; the chances are once again 50-50, because chance has no memory. Audiences usually understand this concept quite well.

But then you ask: In a regular deck of playing cards, what are the chances that the top card would be red? Again, the audience will respond 50-50. This would be a perfect time to begin the finale of the demonstration and flip over the first card in the red pile. The audience will surely think that this was a stroke of luck and nothing more.

You then continue your lesson: But what about the second card? If the first card turned over is red, are the chances still 50-50 the

47

second card will be red? The answer is *no.* The chances are actually *less* that the next card would be red. Why? Well, unlike coins, cards do not have an unlimited supply of heads and tails. When a coin lands on heads, it does not have one less "heads" in its supply. Conversely, there are a limited number of red cards. Once a red card is turned over, there would be an imbalance in the deck, leaving the reds with one less card than the blacks, therefore lowering the chances of the next card being red.

You can ask: So would you all agree that the chances of the second card being red are slightly less than 50-50? You will most likely achieve full agreement from everyone present. What a perfect time to flip over the second card! Now the audience is becoming alarmed. They see two red cards flipped over in a row, but are still thinking it is most likely a coincidence.

You continue: And, of course, once two reds have been used, the odds are *even less* that the next card will be red. You flip over the third red card. At this point, the audience is bracing themselves for a shock beyond their wildest fears. *Is it possible that every one of the cards in that pile is red???*

You continue with your taunting until a few more cards have been drawn. You can conclude by flipping the rest of the red cards over rapidly one by one saying something to the order of: But what would be the odds that *all* the cards in this pile were red???

With bulging eyes and pale faces, your audience will be frozen in their tracks. After a moment, someone will get the brainy idea that maybe the entire deck was red. Instinctively, he will reach for the black pile and turn it over. When they see that all these cards are black, they won't be able to control their horror.

Call 911, get out the first aid kit, and begin CPR. This shock is generally too much for the average human to withstand.

A Great Variation!

Okay, I know what you're thinking. Allow me, if I may, to play out a conversation that we would most likely have if we were together now:

> You: But I don't like presetting cards. It's totally bogus, man.
> Me: I hear you.
> You: This trick stinks.
> Me: You stink.
> You: No, you stink.
> Me: Fine, I stink. I can see that you are clearly upset about having to preset the cards. So here is a variation that eliminates the need for presetting the deck, and still achieves the same effect. Happy now?
> You: Yes.
> Me: Do I still stink?
> You: Not as badly.

In this version, you can have a spectator shuffle the deck to his heart's content. When he is confident that the cards are thoroughly mixed, he hands the deck back to you.

You announce that you will test the audience's power of ESP. To begin, you remove the same four cards as you did in the original version (two reds and two blacks). Place one red card faceup on the table and one black card faceup right next to it (you will save the other two cards for later, as in the previous explanation).

Here's the twist: Fan out the cards in your hand so that they face you and not the audience. Study the deck for a moment, and then pull out a red card. Ask a spectator if she thinks that the card is black or red. If she says red, then place the card facedown in the red pile. If she says black, place the card facedown in the black pile.

You then select another red card, and, without showing it, ask an audience member to identify the color. You then put the card facedown in the appropriate pile. You continue to do this until all the red cards have been removed from the deck.

At this point, there will be only black cards left. It is now time to reverse the deck, as described in the original version. Pick up those other two cards you removed at the beginning of the demonstration (one red, one black), and place the black card faceup on the

49

red pile, and the red card faceup on the black pile (refer back to the diagram on page 42).

You then have two options. You could hand the black cards to a spectator and finish the demonstration as described in the earlier version, since there are only black cards left. Or, if you prefer, you could finish off the black cards the same way as the red.

Once all the cards have been placed, conclude the demonstration as explained previously.

With a little practice, either version of *How Did I Do That?* will be sure to leave your audience wondering *how you did that!*

Psychic-in-Training

DIFFICULTY LEVEL: ✦✦✦✦✦
IMPACT: ✹✹✹✹✹
TECHNIQUE: SLEIGHT OF HAND/ACTING STUPID (TWO VERSIONS)
PREPARATION: NONE

Overview

For those of you who prefer a little playacting with your mind reading, this exhibition will be of particular interest to you. Your role: Playing dumb. Think you can handle it? I know, I know, it's a bit of a stretch, but I think you're up to the challenge.

The mentalist admits to the audience that he is only an apprenticé mind reader, still practicing his craft, trying to earn his way to journeyman status. He asks the audience to bear with him if he doesn't perform all the steps properly.

The Premise

Acting unsure of his abilities, the "apprentice" mind reader stumbles his way through the demonstration, making gaffes and second-guessing himself. In fact, at one point, he actually has to stop his performance because he forgets an important step. Here is how it plays out:

The mind reader writes a prediction on a piece of paper, folds it up, and asks a spectator to insert it anywhere he likes in the deck. Once this is accomplished, the mind reader places the cards on the table and tries to think of the next step. After pausing a moment, he realizes that he left out something important. The mind reader tells the audience that he forgot to instruct the spectator to write his initials on the piece of paper.

51

To remedy this, the mind reader separates the deck where the paper was inserted, so that two piles of cards sit on the table. He then grabs the piece of paper and hands it to the spectator to initial. Once this is done, the mind reader places the piece of paper back on one stack and then covers the paper with the remaining cards. The initialed piece of paper with the prediction written on it is now sandwiched in the deck of cards.

The mind reader apologizes for being so inept and warns the audience that the outcome will probably not be favorable since he is sure that he did something wrong. He says that the goal of this demonstration is to predict where the spectator would insert the paper into the deck. And that if he did his job correctly, the two cards immediately surrounding the paper will match the two cards predicted on the paper.

The mind reader looks very nervous and has his fingers crossed as a spectator opens up the piece of paper and reads the prediction. Another spectator turns over the surrounding cards. The mind reader breathes a heavy sigh of relief when he sees that the cards do indeed match the prediction.

Solution

Essentially, your job is to predict the two cards that will be surrounding the slip of paper inserted into the deck. Since there is no possible way of knowing what those two cards could be, you will have to employ some good old-fashioned trickery to make this work.

After a spectator shuffles the deck, the first thing you will need to do is sneak a peek at two cards: the top card and the bottom card. You may be wondering how you will get away with this indiscretion when the audience is staring at you the whole time. Here is a bold and entertaining method:

After the deck has been shuffled, you announce that you would like to test your newly developed psychic skills and perform a mind reading exhibition. Tell the audience that before you begin, you need to remove the evil king of spades from the deck (more about the king later). What do you have against the king of spades? Well, nothing, actually. You are only inventing this story so you can rummage through the deck and glance at the top and bottom cards!

Memorize these two cards, remove the king of spades from the deck, and then place the deck facedown on the table. Explain to the audience that you will be writing down a prediction on a slip of paper. Letting no one see what you write, jot down the top and bottom cards on the paper. Then fold it up, fold it again, and hand the slip of paper to a spectator.

Pick up the cards and fan them facedown. Ask the spectator to place your prediction anywhere he likes in the deck.

And why must you act like an idiot for this demonstration to work? Well, the first reason is because it is a lot of fun to pretend that things are going poorly when you know very well that the trick will work like a charm. The second reason is to justify why you "forgot" to have the paper initialized. If you appear genuine, the audience will assume that you have not fully practiced this routine and need to work out some of the kinks.

Now we've come to the crucial part. Pay close attention to these instructions and you will pull it off like a pro. Allow me to break it down into five easy steps.

Step 1: Tell the audience that you forgot to have the paper initialized. If they ask why this is important, say it is because you do not want to be accused of switching papers.

Step 2: Separate the deck at the point where the paper was inserted. Take the top stack of cards and place it to the right of the remainder of the deck. So now there are two piles of cards. The pile to the left has the folded slip of paper resting on top (see drawing).

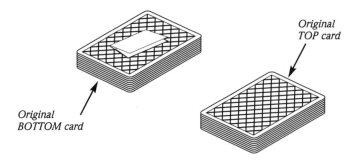

Original
TOP card

Original
BOTTOM card

Keep in mind that the top card on the stack on the right *is the original top card* at which you peeked earlier. Think about it.

53

The order of the cards never changed, and this card is now resting comfortably on top of the pile on the right. By the same token, remember that the bottom card under the stack on the left *is the original bottom card* at which you peeked earlier.

Step 3: Hand the slip of paper to the spectator and ask him to initial it. Once he does this, take the paper back from him.

Step 4: While you explain the importance of having the paper initialized, you *place the piece of paper on top of the stack on the right.* Hey, wait a minute! That isn't where it's supposed to go! If you wanted to put the paper back where the spectator originally placed it, then you would have put it on the left pile and not the right.

Let's face it. You do not want to put the paper back where the spectator placed it. Instead, you want to place it on top of the pile on the right. Here's why:

Step 5: Take the stack of cards on the left pile, and place them on top of the cards on the right pile. The slip of paper will now be sandwiched between the two stacks, *surrounded by the original top and bottom cards!*

And now the prediction written on the paper will match the surrounding cards exactly. If you practice this with a deck of cards, you will see that it makes perfect sense.

Tips & Techniques

Let's first talk about the removal of the king of spades at the beginning of the demonstration. As I mentioned, you will explain to the audience that your psychic skills are still developing, and you do not possess the powers to overcome certain powerful elements that reside in a deck of cards. The most formidable foe to any mind reader is the king of spades. It is this king's job to protect the other cards and block extrasensory powers from penetrating the deck. Once it is removed, you will be able to conduct the demonstration unimpeded.

Why on earth will the audience accept the fact that you need to remove the king from the deck? They won't, but in most cases, this deception throws them off the track completely. They usually furrow their brows trying to figure out what the king of spades has to do with this demonstration. Let them think what they want. All you care about is catching a glimpse of the top and bottom cards.

The other part of the demonstration that needs to be executed flawlessly is the move at the end when you switch the two halves of the deck. Without appearing rushed, this move must be performed quickly and nonchalantly. Look your spectators in the eye as you execute the move, and talk to them about why you need to have the prediction initialized. It is to assure the audience that the paper will not be switched. By the time you finish your explanation, the move will have been made, and you can then take your time with a dramatic finish.

Remember not to mention what it is you are trying to predict until after the switch has been made. You don't want your audience on the lookout for any funny business with the deck until you have finished manipulating it. At this point, the audience already has much to think about: the evil king of spades, the piece of paper in the deck, the initials on the paper. There are so many deceptions to throw them off course, they will not be aware of your pile switching evil.

Here's another tip that will avoid some potential problems: When you ask the spectator to insert the paper anywhere he wants in the deck, impress upon him that you are not attempting to "force" him into placing it in any particular spot. Tell him to take his time and place the paper only where he is most comfortable.

It will not be to your advantage, however, if he places the paper too close to either end of the deck. This is because when you separate the deck into two piles, one stack will be significantly larger than the other, and it may be more noticeable that you are placing the paper on the wrong portion of the deck.

Here's how to combat this: After explaining that the spectator has the freedom to place the paper anywhere he likes, say "Except there." This will usually generate some laughter. Suggest that he stick closer toward the middle of the deck.

Switcheroo!

10

DIFFICULTY LEVEL: ◆◆◆◆◆
IMPACT: ✴✴✴✴✴
TECHNIQUE: SLEIGHT OF HAND (PARTNER REQUIRED FOR MAIN VERSION)
PREPARATION: VERY LITTLE

Overview

Mind reading demonstrations that involve the telephone are among the most baffling ever conceived. Audiences are astonished when they hear someone at another location identify a card that was just selected. Most of these demonstrations require the mind reader to call a "wizard" and provide cleverly concealed clues to reveal a secret card. A spectator then gets on the telephone to hear the wizard name the correct card. Although quite spectacular, the problem with these demonstrations is that the audience generally assumes that some sort of code is being transmitted.

But what if you could perform a feat using the telephone where the mind reader never speaks to the wizard? If this were possible, then the mind reader could not be accused of using a code or signaling system. I invented *Switcheroo!* to do just that. In this demonstration, it is an audience member who speaks to the wizard over the telephone. The mind reader is merely a spectator watching the demonstration unfold.

The Premise

The mind reader announces to the audience that she knows of a wizard who is able to make incredible predictions over the telephone. To prove this, she produces a deck of cards. An observer is invited to mix the cards thoroughly. Once this is done, the mind reader asks the observer to fan out the cards on a table.

Another observer is asked to pick out a card without looking at it. This observer places the card facedown on the table. The mind reader then picks up the remaining cards and puts them in her pocket. The only card remaining on the table is the one chosen by the observer. Since the card is facedown, no one (not even the mind reader) knows what it is.

The mind reader writes down the wizard's name and telephone number on a piece of paper, and hands it to another observer. The mind reader then picks up the selected card (being very careful NOT to look at it) and folds it in half, then in half again. She asks a volunteer to hand her an envelope from the table and places the folded card inside. She then seals the envelope and hands it to another observer.

At this point, no one has seen the card. It has been folded twice and sealed inside an envelope. It is being carefully guarded by an audience member, so that the mind reader cannot tamper with it.

The mind reader then asks the observer with the telephone number to call the wizard and ask the identity of the card. The wizard will attempt to identify the card in the envelope.

After the wizard predicts the card, the observer hangs up the telephone and announces the prediction to the crowd. Now we have to see whether this prediction matches the card in the envelope. (Wouldn't it be amazing if it does?) The observer holding the envelope is asked to open it and remove the card. The card is unfolded and revealed to the audience. *Voilà!* A perfect match.

Solution

There is some simple preparation required for this demonstration. These are all very easy tasks, so I don't want to hear complaining from any of you (you heard me). You will need to do the following before you begin:

- Ask a friend you can trust to help you with a fun demonstration. Tell this friend that someone will be calling him on the telephone at approximately 9:00 that night to ask for the identity of a card. When this happens, instruct your friend to say the **jack of clubs.**

- Remove the jack of clubs from a deck of cards, fold it in half, then in half again. Before you begin the demonstration, place this card in your hand, snugly concealed by your ring finger and middle finger (practice this; most of it should fit in there easily).
- Place the remainder of the deck on the table, along with an envelope, a pen, and a piece of paper.

Now you are ready to start. As you may have guessed from the folded-up card under your ring finger and middle finger, the solution relies on a sleight of hand movement. Let's briefly walk through the steps in the demonstration so you can see where the maneuver takes place. It is very important that these steps take place in this exact order:

- A deck is thoroughly shuffled by a spectator as the mind reader explains the premise.
- One card is selected at random by a spectator and put aside (with no one seeing the card).
- The mind reader gathers up the remaining cards and places them in her pocket.
- The wizard's telephone number is written on a piece of paper and handed to an observer.

Here is the big move:

- The mind reader folds the selected card in half, then in half again—in plain view of the audience (the mind reader not looking at the card). She holds this card between her thumb and pointer (in the same hand that she has the jack of clubs hidden). She then asks a spectator to hand her the envelope that is on the table. *The mind reader uses her thumb to switch the two cards in her hand. She then places the folded-up jack of clubs in the envelope* (see *Tips & Techniques* for help in completing this maneuver).

And the demonstration plays out as described above:

- The envelope is sealed and handed to an observer.
- The observer with the telephone number calls the wizard and asks the identity of the card; then the card is announced to the audience.
- The observer guarding the envelope opens it and reveals the card.

Tips & Techniques

How easy is it to switch the cards? Like anything else, with some practice you can become quite good at it. There are two things to consider when making the switch. First and foremost, you must distract the audience momentarily. Second, the switch must be made quickly. Let's examine both of these areas more closely.

Distracting the Audience

So, here you are at a party, performing this mind-reading feat for your family and closest friends. You're in the middle of the demonstration about to make the old switcheroo. You have the jack of clubs folded up nicely under your ring finger and middle finger. The card that an observer selected is folded up and held between your thumb and pointer in the same hand. Can you picture it? Sweat is dripping from your brow, and your heart is pounding through your chest. Time to make the switch!

Remember that envelope you placed on the table when you were setting up the demonstration? Well, now is the time to put it to use. You point to the table with your free hand and say, "Can someone please hand me that envelope?" Here is your chance! For an instant, the audience will divert their focus to the envelope on the table. The switch takes only a fraction of a second and will be fully executed by the time they look back.

I have found that when the audience looks away (oh, and they will), there is so much time to make the switch, you do not have to rush. I am not suggesting you can waste time, but if you relax and casually execute the switch, you will have a much greater chance at success than if you hurry through it.

The Switch

The first thing you need to do is to practice holding the folded-up card (the jack of clubs) under your ring finger and middle finger. The card has been folded twice so that it will fit snugly in place. You need to feel comfortable keeping these fingers bent since they will be in this position during the entire demonstration. If you try this you will see that these two fingers do not have to be bent over all the way, just far enough to hold the card and conceal it from the audience. This is not an unusual position to hold your hand, and you will find that gesturing with this hand will still appear quite natural.

If you prefer, you can try folding the card a third time and see if that feels more comfortable. If you do this, just make sure that you fold the selected card the same way.

I will explain the easiest way I know to make the switch, but with practice, you can develop your own method. You can perfect this technique by trying it one day for ten or fifteen minutes. It just takes a few practice tries to get used to it.

In order to understand this move, it is essential that you try it as you read through this explanation:

The observer's card is held between your thumb and pointer. Slide this card downward with your thumb. You must position it in your hand so that it slides *over* the jack of clubs that you have tucked away under your ring finger and middle finger. Keep sliding it until it is past the jack of clubs, then latch onto it with your pinky. Once your pinky has a nice grip on the card, simply use your thumb to slide the jack of clubs up to your pointer. Hold the jack between your thumb and pointer.

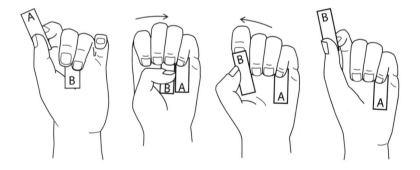

When an observer hands you the envelope, place the jack of clubs inside, seal the envelope, and hand it back to him for safe keeping. At your first opportunity, drop the other folded card you have in your hand into one of your pockets.

60

Other Tips

- When you hand the observer the sealed envelope that contains the jack of clubs, go ahead and make a big deal of the responsibility you are bestowing upon her. Let her know that she is the protector of the secret card and should do everything in her power to make sure that no one gets a glimpse of the envelope's contents until the end of the demonstration. No matter how much people beg and plead, she must not open the envelope until she is instructed to do so.

- When a spectator calls the wizard on the telephone to ask the identity of the card in the envelope, leave it entirely up to the audience to decide how the question will be posed. If you tell the spectator how to phrase the question, you will be accused of sending a secret signal to your partner.

- If you want to take this one step further, you could use Caller ID technology to aid you in this demonstration. Tell your partner the telephone number of the person you are visiting that evening. This way, when he sees the number appear on his Caller ID, he can simply answer the telephone, pause, and then name the card—without even saying hello!

- There's still one very important aspect of the demonstration that I have yet to discuss. I recommend you keep a second deck of cards in your jacket pocket. This deck will be identical to the first, except that the jack of clubs is missing. Here's why: Suppose you successfully perform the demonstration and your audience is rolling around on the floor in agony, yanking their hair from its roots, trying to figure out how you achieved this feat of wizardry. At some point a spectator might suggest the possibility that you may have indeed pulled the old switcheroo and put a different card in the envelope. (Can you believe how suspicious people are?)

   If an audience member suspects this, he may ask to inspect the deck. Consider this: If you did indeed switch cards (and let's face it, you did), that would mean that there would be *two* cards missing from the deck: The jack of clubs and the card that the spectator actually selected. So if a spectator insists on inspecting the deck, he would discover two cards missing and, therefore, the secret of the demonstration. Even if you manage to sneak the card the spectator chose back into the deck, it would be badly bent from being folded—a dead giveaway.

This is where the second deck will come in handy. Remember, after a spectator selects a card and pulls it from the deck, you will immediately gather up the remaining cards and put them in your pocket. You then continue with the demonstration as described earlier. At any point during the demonstration, all you have to do is take out the second deck from your pocket and place it on the table. A great time to do this is when a spectator is calling the wizard. People will be paying attention to the person dialing the telephone. By the way, once the deck is replaced, you can easily "prove" that you used an ordinary deck of cards by challenging the audience to inspect, count, and verify the cards in the deck.

What if you don't like using a second deck? No problem. You can accomplish the same result by keeping an extra card (from a similar deck) hidden in your pocket. After the spectator selects a card, you put the rest of the deck in your pocket right next to the extra card. This way, when you remove the deck later, there will be the appropriate number of cards in the deck. I have seen people count the deck after a demonstration, but I have *never* seen them go through all of the suits and numbers to make sure they were all accounted for.

• Once the sleight has been performed, you can breathe a sigh of relief and have fun with the conclusion. When the wizard is called and asked to identify the card in the envelope, encourage the spectator to help out by rubbing the envelope on the telephone receiver, doing a "psychic card dance," or even humming the theme to Jeopardy. If your partner is also a weirdo, he can instruct the spectator over the telephone to perform any number of hilarious acts to help him identify the card.

Another Version

Don't have any friends who will give you their telephone number? I hear you. I'm in the same boat. Here is a version for those of you who do not wish to include any friends in your performance.

In this version, no pencil or paper is needed. Follow the instructions exactly as before—up to and including the step where you pull the switch and place the jack of clubs in the envelope. Once the envelope has been sealed, you can use your own psychic abilities to reveal the identity of the card.

Since you already know the identity of the card in the envelope, you can be as creative as you like in unleashing your mystical powers. Use your imagination; the sky's the limit. Whatever you do at this point will not affect the final result, so have fun! Here are a few suggestions:

- Pour salt on the envelope and rub it around while chanting the theme to your favorite sit-com.
- Ask members of the audience to sniff the envelope and say what reptile it reminds them of.
- Take out a calculator, and appear as if you are solving a complex mathematical calculation.

If you want, you can actually use this silliness in place of the sleight of hand described above. Instead of switching cards before sealing the envelope, you could put the original card in the envelope and then *switch envelopes* while you are monkeying around later. You can use any method you like to switch envelopes. Here is just one example:

During your psychic frenzy, place the envelope in a telephone book, and then pass the book around the audience, asking them to whisper their middle names into the book. When the book circulates back to you, open the book to a different page and remove the secret envelope containing the jack of clubs that you had preset before beginning the demonstration.

11

What's Your Number?

DIFFICULTY LEVEL: ✦✦✦✦✦

IMPACT: ✳✳✳✳✳

TECHNIQUE: EVIL MATHEMATICS/PRESET DECK

PREPARATION: MINIMAL

Overview

Some tricks have such earth-shattering impact that they stick with spectators for many years to come. What makes this demonstration so unfathomable is that it involves something personal.

I will teach you the solution to this miracle under one condition: You must promise never to perform it. It is for educational purposes only. The human mind was not designed to absorb the impact caused by witnessing this maddening exhibition of sheer mental power.

I saw this demonstration performed by master magician Joel Lerner at a private affair on a recent Thanksgiving. The effect was so stunning that it left a deep impression on every spectator for several months. If he were able to turn our turkey dinner into the ten of spades, it would not have been as impressive as this remarkable psychic feat. Mr. Lerner was kind enough to share his closely guarded secret for the enjoyment of my readers.

This will be your show stopper, the *pièce de résistance,* et cetera et cetera. Save this demonstration for last. This is the one you perform just as you are leaving the party. You want to bring your audience to their knees? You want to leave them stupefied? Then learn this demonstration. This trick alone is worth the price of the book, whatever it is. In fact, it is so mind-boggling, I think you should pay a little extra to learn it. Before you read any further, go back to store and give them some more money. I'll wait.

The Premise

Back? Okay, here we go!

Step 1: The mind reader selects five volunteers to sit around a table with him and participate in an exhibition of mental telepathy. He shows the deck, faceup, to his audience, to prove that it is a random, legitimate deck of cards.

Step 2: The mind reader then fans the cards facedown, and asks the first spectator to select a card. Once the spectator looks at it, he is asked whether he is happy with his selection. If he is, then he keeps the card. If not, he is allowed to replace it in the deck and select another card.

The mind reader repeats this process three more times, until four of the five spectators have selected a card from the deck. The fifth volunteer is appointed the dealer, and is handed the rest of the cards.

Step 3: Let's assume that the spectators picked the following cards:

4 of Hearts   7 of Spades   King of Clubs   8 of Hearts

In this demonstration, *the suits are completely meaningless.*

The first spectator is asked to place his card faceup on the table. The mind reader then explains that piles will be made in front of each of the four cards that were selected. Each pile needs to total ten.

What do I mean by that? Well, let's look at the first card—the four of hearts. To total ten, six more cards must be placed in front of the four, *facedown* (since four plus six equal ten). It does not matter what the cards are; the only thing that matters is that the dealer places six cards in front of the four.

The mind reader then instructs the second spectator to turn over his card—the 7 of spades. He asks the audience how many cards need to be added to the seven of spades to equal ten. There is always one math genius in the crowd who will know that the correct answer is three, since seven plus three equals ten. At that point, the dealer will place the appropriate number of cards in front of the seven (facedown). Again, it doesn't matter what the cards are, as long as three more are dealt.

The next spectator turns over his card—the king of clubs—and places it on the table. The mind reader states that all tens,

65

jacks, queens, and kings count as ten. Since the pile already equals ten, there is no need to add any cards to it.

Finally, the last spectator places his card on the table—the eight of hearts. By now the audience will have caught on to the procedure and will know that only two cards need to be piled in front of the eight (facedown) to total ten.

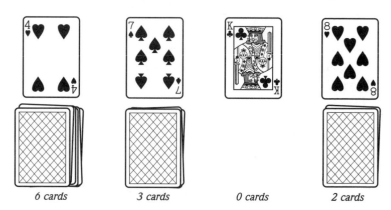

| 6 cards | 3 cards | 0 cards | 2 cards |

Step 3: The mind reader then asks the dealer to gather the facedown cards and put them *underneath the remaining deck.* The only cards that should remain on the table are the four original cards that were selected by the volunteers (the four of hearts, seven of spades, king of clubs, and eight of hearts).

Step 4: One of the volunteers is asked to then *add up* the value of the four cards. Let's try that, shall we?

$4 + 7 + 10$ (king) $+ 8 = $ **29**.

Step 5: The dealer is then asked to count off **29** cards from the top of the deck. Obviously, this total will vary depending upon which cards are selected by the volunteers. Once these cards are counted off the deck, they are put to the side.

Step 6: The mind reader explains that the very next card turned over will be the "magic number." The dealer turns over a seven (yes, it will always be a seven; you'll see why later).

Step 7: Acting surprised to see a seven, the mind reader scratches his head and ponders the situation for a moment. After reflecting, he says this means that seven cards should be dealt faceup on the table, all in a row. The dealer places the seven cards in a row, as instructed.

66

The mind reader then pauses and lets the audience look at the seven cards displayed in front of them to see if they have any significance. After a minute or so, there will be a gasp, which is usually followed by someone shrieking, *"Oh my God! That's my phone number!!!"*

Solution

Not possible, you say? I know. It was inconceivable to me how *my* telephone number was spelled out in front of me. I replayed every one of the mind reader's movements in my head over and over for several weeks, and still I could not figure out how he pulled this off.

The first thing you need to know is that eight cards must be pre-set at the bottom of the deck before the demonstration begins. These eight cards are as follows:

A seven (any suit) and a spectator's telephone number (placed underneath the seven). These will be the bottom eight cards in the deck. Now, let's turn to the solution that makes this demonstration possible.

The answer, of course, is evil mathematics. Yes, the same branch of science that brought you $2 + 2 = 4$ is responsible for this unfathomable masterpiece. The solution is straightforward. If you follow the instructions written in the premise, the demonstration is foolproof. Here is a review of the key points:

- Four cards are selected by audience members.
- Cards are piled in front of each card to equal ten.
- The value of the four cards is added. In our example, the total was 29.
- The dealer counts off this many cards from the top of the deck.

Here is the mathematical formula:

The total value of the four cards + the amount of cards dealt onto the piles = 40.

Let me say it again:

The total value of the four cards + the amount of cards dealt onto the piles = 40.

To see whether this is accurate, let's examine our example:

4 of Hearts   7 of Spades   King of Clubs   8 of Hearts

We already know that the value of these four cards equals 29 because:

4 + 7 + 10 + 8 = 29

But how many cards were piled in front of these original four cards to equal ten?

Well, we added:

6 cards to the 4
3 cards to the 7
0 cards to the king
2 cards to the 8
_____

11 is our total.

And **29 + 11 = 40.**

But does this work every time? It sure does. Rather than give you example after example of how *any* four cards will generate the same results, I will leave it up to you to do your own experiments later. For now, please give me the benefit of the doubt so I can move on and explain the significance of this mathematical oddity.

No? You won't do that for me? Okay then. Let's try one more example:

6 of Spades   2 of Hearts   Queen of Clubs   4 of Diamonds

The total value of these cards is: **6 + 2 + 10 + 4 = 22**

How many cards do we need to add to each card to equal ten?

4 cards to the 6
8 cards to the 2
0 cards to the 10
6 cards to the 4
_____

18 is our total.

And **22 + 18 = 40.**

Satisfied? May I move on now? Thank you.

So, what is the big deal about the number 40, you ask? Consider this:

The deck started with **52** cards. Four cards were selected initially, bringing the total now remaining in the deck to **48**. As we just discovered, an additional **40** cards were dealt and counted off, leaving only **8** cards left from the original 52. Because:

52 − 4 − 40 = 8

And just what do you suppose those eight remaining cards are? *They are the eight cards you preset before you started the demonstration.* As noted in the premise, the first of those eight cards is a 7. This "magic card" tells you how many cards need to be dealt. You instruct the dealer to deal this many cards faceup on the table, all in a row. Ask the audience if they can see any significance in the cards that were dealt. It will only take a moment for someone to realize that she is looking at her telephone number.

If you're half as exhausted from reading this explanation as I am from writing it, then you'll probably need to take a little nap. I'll see you in *Tips & Techniques* after you have rested.

Tips & Techniques

 Welcome back. I trust you had a pleasant sleep. Now, let's get back to business.

It is important for you to have a complete understanding of how this demonstration is performed before progressing further. If any part is unclear, reread the solution while you follow along with a deck of cards.

One of the chief reasons that this demonstration is so baffling is because after the spectators select their initial card, the mind reader does not handle the deck. As people reflect back on the moves of the mind reader, they will not be able to accuse him of slipping the telephone number into the deck during the demonstration. Once he hands the cards to the dealer, he can sit back and watch the demonstration unfold.

As always, the audience wants to be certain that the deck is thoroughly mixed. Since we are working with a preset deck, shuffling the cards is not an option. To combat this objection, you can go one step further: Fan the cards out in your hands faceup, letting the audience see that it is indeed a full deck and that the cards are different from one another. This is a great technique that usually puts the audience's suspicions to rest.

If you are careful, you can casually shuffle the cards once or twice while introducing the demonstration, as long as the eight preset cards remain undisturbed at the bottom of the deck.

Other Tips

- When it is time for the volunteers to select their cards from the deck, you will fan the cards out facedown. It is important to bunch the preset eight cards together so that it is impossible for a spectator to select one of them. The fact that the volunteers are free to exchange their cards adds a nice touch to an already baffling feat. It emphasizes the random element of the demonstration, and reduces the risk of spectators thinking the deck was preset.

- What if you want to perform this demonstration for less than five people? No problem. Simply have your volunteers select more than one card each (making sure that only four cards are drawn). This exhibition works best for small groups, but, if necessary, can even be performed for just one spectator.

- It is important that when the cards in the piles are gathered, they are then placed underneath the remaining deck. If this doesn't happen, then the dealer will be holding only eight cards in his hand when the demonstration has concluded. The impact is far greater if it appears as if the telephone number is sandwiched somewhere in the middle of the deck, rather than at the bottom of the deck.

- Whose telephone number should you use? It is best to select someone who is known by most of the audience. This way they can corroborate that the telephone number is correct. I like to choose someone whom I do not know very well. It only takes one minute of preparation to look up a telephone number. When I know there is a possibility that I will be performing this demonstration at a party or function, I preselect a person before I arrive. This way I have the telephone number memorized and can be ready to begin at any time.

    Ideally, you will arrange the demonstration so that the owner of the telephone number will end up being the dealer. The easiest way to accomplish this is to ask the volunteers who wants to be the "mark" at the beginning of the demonstration. If your target should volunteer for this, tell him that he will be designated as the dealer. If someone else volunteers, allow him to select a card from the deck first. Then ask again. One way or another, you will usually be able to manipulate your audience into making your target the dealer.

• What if there is a zero in the person's telephone number? You may have noticed that there are no zero of clubs or zero of diamonds in the deck. What will you do? An easy solution is to mention that for this part of the demo, picture cards can count as zeros.

• The finale of this demonstration is so spectacular because the audience has no idea what to expect. You can enhance the impact by pretending that you are not exactly sure how the demonstration is supposed to be performed. This way, when the telephone number is revealed, you can act just as surprised as your audience to discover this astonishing miracle.

Sometimes it takes a few minutes for the audience to realize that they are looking at someone's telephone number. If this takes longer than expected, coach the spectators along until they realize what they are seeing. Ask an audience member to read the numbers out loud. Usually hearing one's telephone number recited is enough to spark a hint of recognition.

• What if the audience asks you to perform this demonstration again? Should you? Absolutely not! You've gotten away with it once; the second time you may not be as lucky. Save *What's Your Number* for special occasions only. It is bound to be one of the very best mental feats in your repertoire.

Telepathy for Two

12

DIFFICULTY LEVEL: ◆◆◆◆◆
IMPACT: ✹✹✹✹✹
TECHNIQUE: CODES/PARTNER
PREPARATION: EXTENSIVE REHEARSAL

Overview

If you would like to be considered a major player in the mind-reading field, then I strongly suggest you take the time to learn *Telepathy for Two*. It is a spectacular feat of mind reading that never fails to stump even the most critical audiences. This demonstration is so bewildering because the spectators are free to inspect the cards, the magician never handles the deck, and it can be performed multiple times by using slight variations. And (get this!), the mind reader is not even in the room when a spectator is asked to select a card! Did that grab your attention? Read on to learn this amusing and baffling technique.

The Premise

The mind reader hands a deck of cards to an audience member and asks him to inspect and mix it thoroughly. While the shuffling is taking place, the mind reader announces to the crowd that he has the ability to read minds, and has devised a demonstration to prove it. He states that he is about to leave the room momentarily while a volunteer selects a card from the meticulously shuffled deck. When he returns to the room, he will announce the card to the audience. Too good to be true? See for yourself ...

Solution

I am about to teach you the answer to this mind-blowing, supernatural feat, but it will require a little work on your end. (I mean, I can't do everything for you!) The solution is a virtually undetectable code that you will practice with a partner.

Wouldn't it be great if there were only ten cards in the deck? This way you could work out a separate signal with your partner for each and every card. Then again, with only ten cards, the trick wouldn't be as spectacular.

Because we have 52 cards, it would not be practical or fun to create a code that used a separate signal for each card. With *Telepathy for Two* you will use a system that breaks the clues into groups. I'm going to explain, in great detail, how the clue system works. Although it takes several pages to describe, you only have to memorize four clues.

The first clue you will receive from your partner will indicate the color of the card and then the suit. First let's address the color. While you are out of the room, your partner will give you a signal that the card has been selected, and you should return to the room. *This signal is your clue.*

CLUE #1

If your partner says, "We're ready," this lets you know that the card is black. If your partner says anything else, then the card is red.

Does that sound simple enough so far? Just by being called back into the room, you have already identified the color of the card.

Each color, by the way, has a *dominant* suit. Spade is the dominant black suit and heart is the dominant red suit.

Dominant = Spade, Heart

Non-Dominant = Club, Diamond

This will help you decipher the second part of the clue—the suit. If the card is a dominant suit, your partner will say "Okay" when calling you back into the room. So, "Okay, we're ready" means it is a spade. Why? Because:

"We're ready" = black card

"Okay" = dominant suit (since it is a black card, the suit is spade)

Conversely, if you heard "Come on back in," you will know that the card is red (because your partner did not say "we're ready"), and since your partner did not say "okay," you know that it is the non-dominant suit, which is diamonds.

"Come on back in" (or anything other than "we're ready") = red card

No "okay" = non-dominant suit (since it is a red card, the suit is diamond)

See how much fun this will be? With just one clue, you have already determined the suit! Hold on to your seats, because it gets a little more complicated.

When you re-enter the room, you are ready for your next clue. But before you receive this clue, you will tease the audience by announcing the color of the card (you'll see why in a second). Let's assume that the **nine of clubs** has been chosen. Since you already know the suit, you can safely declare to the spectators, "I know that the color of the chosen card is black."

You're off to a good start! But you know audiences; they are never satisfied with just the color. To impress them you're going to have to reveal the number and suit of the card. As you have just learned, however, you already know the suit and will reveal it in a moment.

To discover the number of the card, we need to narrow it down a little further. Let's break down the cards into smaller groups. Since you know the suit, we can limit our choices to just thirteen cards. If we disregard the ace (see "Tips & Techniques" later in the chapter for tips on the ace), we have twelve cards left, or two groups of six cards. Let's break the groups down as follows:

Top Half: 8 9 10 Jack Queen King
Bottom Half: 2 3 4 5 6 7

The next thing you want to know is whether the chosen card is in the top half (eight through king) or in the bottom half (two through seven). You will make that determination in the next clue. After you say, *"I know that the color of the chosen card is black,"* your partner gives you the following signal:

CLUE #2

If the card is in the top half of the deck, your partner says something (anything!). If the card is in the bottom half, your partner says *nothing*.

That's right. Even silence is a clue, which is why this code is practically undetectable.

74

Since our card is a nine of clubs, your partner will say something (such as "that's correct" or "yes"). From his signal, you know that the card is in the top half of the deck (eight through king). Now it is time to narrow it down even further.

Let's break down these six cards in the top half into two groups of three:

Jack Queen King (upper part)

8 9 10 (lower part)

(FYI: If the bottom half of the deck had been selected, the two groups would have been 2 3 4 and 5 6 7).

Before you receive this clue, you must first tell the audience the suit. You will say, "Not only do I know that the card is black, but I also know it is a club!" Here's where the next clue comes in:

CLUE #3

If the card is in the upper three (jack, queen, king), your partner will say something (again, anything at all!). If the card is in the lower three (8, 9, 10), he says nothing.

Since the card is a nine of clubs, your partner will remain silent, letting you know that it is an 8, 9, or 10. Well, there's only one more clue left to let you know the exact card.

Before you receive this last clue, you must first say, "I know the card is not a picture card." (Of course it's not; you know it has to be an 8, 9, or 10. Conversely, if you had determined that it was a picture card, you would say so.) Your partner then gives you the final clue:

CLUE #4

If the card is the *first* one in the grouping (the eight), he says nothing. If it is the *second* card in the grouping (the nine), he says only one word (such as "right" or "yes"). If it is the *highest* card in the grouping (the ten) he says more than one word (such as "What's the card?" or "Tell us what it is.").

Since the card is a nine, your partner will say just one word, letting you know that the card is the second in the grouping—the nine of clubs. You announce this to the crowd, and take all the credit for yourself—even though it was your partner who did all the work.

Review

Yes, it sounds a bit complicated, but when you consider that it is only four basic clues that your partner gives, it is actually a very learnable code. Note: You always know more than you are revealing to the audience. Try not to let that throw you! The following chart gives you a handy guide to practice the clues:

CLUE #1 **Determining Card Color**

We're ready = Black Card
Come in now (or anything else besides "we're ready") = Red Card

Determining Suit

Okay = Dominant Suit (Spade or Heart)
No "Okay" = Non-Dominant Suit (Club or Diamond)

> **After hearing this clue,** *you reveal the color of the card* (not the whole suit!)

CLUE #2 **Determining Top Half (eight through king)**
or Bottom Half (two through seven)

Saying Something = Top Half (eight through king)
Silence = Bottom Half (two through seven)

> **After hearing this clue,** *you reveal the suit.*

CLUE #3 **Determining Upper Three**
or Lower Three

Saying Something: = Upper Part (jack, queen, king for top half;
    5, 6, 7 for bottom half)
Silence = Lower Part (8, 9, 10 for top half; 2, 3, 4 for bottom half)

> **After hearing this clue,** *you reveal whether or not it is a picture card.*

CLUE #4 **Determining Number in a Series**

Silence = First number in series (2, 5, 8, or Jack)
One Word = Second number in series (3, 6, 9, or queen)
Two Words or More = Third number in series (4, 7, 10, or king)

> **After hearing this clue,** *you reveal the selected card.*

Still confused? Then take a look at a typical exchange to reveal the **ten of spades:**

Partner: **(Clue #1)** Okay, we're ready. (We're ready = black card; okay = spade)

Mind Reader: I know it is a black card.

Partner: **(Clue #2)** Correct. (Saying something indicates the card is in the top half of the deck—eight through king)

Mind Reader: It is a spade.

Partner: **(Clue #3)** *Silence.* (Saying nothing indicates it is in the bottom three of the top half—8, 9, or 10)

Mind Reader: I can tell that it is not a picture card. (Of course it's not. You've determined that it is an eight, nine, or ten).

Partner: **(Clue #4)** What's the card? (Saying more than one word = highest card in that series, which is a ten).

Mind Reader: The card is a ten of spades.

Do you get it? All it takes is a little practice and you will have the code down pat. Once you master the technical part, it is time to "sell it" to the crowd with a touch of showmanship. See *Tips & Techniques* below for entertaining performance ideas.

Tips & Techniques:

- What if the card is an ace? As you may have noticed, there is no room for an ace anywhere in the code. Should you just hope that no one ever selects an ace? Not at all. In fact, if you are ever so fortunate to have an audience member pick an ace, the demonstration is greatly simplified.

  If an ace is selected, your partner will incorporate it into the first clue by *using your name.* The rest of the clue remains the same, so that you will know the correct suit. So when you hear your name, you know the card is an ace.
- Okay, Bill, we're ready = Ace of Spades
- Bill, we're ready = Ace of Clubs
- Okay, Bill, come in = Ace of Hearts
- Come in, Bill = Ace of Diamonds

  The only problem you may encounter with this code is if your name is not Bill. If that is the case, you may want to consider a name change.

77

This will cut out many steps, and appear as if you just performed a miracle. Imagine if your partner simply said, "Okay, Bill, we're ready," and you come sauntering into the room, naming the card immediately. The audience will think that you are a psychic freak of nature.

- Besides aces, the best cards are twos. This is because most of the clues to reveal a two are silent. Silent clues make it look as if there's no code whatsoever. For example, if the card was a two of clubs, all your partner would have to say is "We're ready," and you will work your way through to the two of clubs without any other verbal assistance. To reveal a two of clubs, the exchange would be as follows:

Partner: **(Clue #1)** We're ready. (We're ready = black card; no okay = club)
Mind Reader: I know it is a black card.
Partner: **(Clue #2)** *Silence.* (Saying nothing indicates the card is in the bottom half of the deck—two through seven)
Mind Reader: It is a club.
Partner: **(Clue #3)** *Silence.* (Saying nothing indicates it is in the lower three of the bottom half—2, 3, or 4)
Mind Reader: I can tell that it is not a picture card. (Of course it's not. You've determined that it is a 2, 3, or 4.)
Partner: **(Clue #4)** *Silence.* (Saying nothing indicates the lowest card in the series, which is a 2).
Mind Reader: The card is a two of clubs.

Did you see what happened? After "We're ready," all subsequent clues were silent.

- At the end, why is a one-word clue used for the *second* item in the list and not the first? Because the *silent* clue has always been associated with the bottom option (*bottom* half, *lower* part, and *lowest* card in a series). If you prefer to switch it, feel free; however, I find it easier keeping the silent clues consistent.

- Do not look at your partner when working through the clues. Since hardly any words are spoken, people might assume that the clues are being transmitted through gestures or posture.

- It is essential that your partner acts as casually as possible.

If it appears that he is transmitting clues, people will suspect that you are using a code. The partner's limited responses must be natural and nonchalant.

- Since you will undoubtedly be asked to perform this trick over and over again, you will want to devise an alternate system that changes the words slightly. You can create a phrase to replace "we're ready," and then keep using different words during the demonstration to keep the audience off balance.

Advanced Method—Watch Out!

Depending upon the amount of practice time and the skill level of you and your partner, it is possible to use an advanced clue system that would cut down on the number of steps needed to identify the card. This method is feasible only if you and your partner have a complete understanding of the demonstration. If not, it will seem far too confusing to attempt. But, for those brave enough to try, you will find the payoff well worth your time.

As it stands now, four clues are required to identify the card. By using some of the following suggestions, you could reduce the number of required clues to two or three. As you have just learned, once you are called into the room, you have already figured out the suit. The rest of the demonstration is altered as follows:

- If the card is in the top half of the deck, your partner crosses his right leg over his left; if it is in the bottom half, the left leg is crossed over the right. This maneuver completely eliminates the need for Clue #2 (above). If you prefer, you can use hands instead of legs.

79

• If your partner is smiling, that means the card is in the upper three (jack, queen, king for top half; 5, 6, 7 for the bottom half); if your partner is not smiling, the card is in the lower three (8, 9, 10 for the upper half and 2, 3, 4 for the lower half). This step eliminates the need for Clue #3 (above).

Example: If your partner calls you into the room by saying, "We're ready," and you notice that his left leg is over his right, and he has a bright smile on his face, you can assume:

The card is black (We're ready = black card)

The card is a club (No "okay" = non-dominant suit, a club)

The card is in the bottom half of the deck, a two through seven (Left leg over the right = bottom half)

The card is in the upper part, 5, 6, or 7 (Smiling = upper three).

So, using this method, your partner said only two words, and you have narrowed down the field from 52 cards to just three.

Are you ready for **total insanity?** You can actually pinpoint the selected card by using one last non-verbal clue. Simply take a look at your partner's left hand and notice how many fingers he is showing. He will easily be able to rest his hand on a table or his knee without anyone suspecting he is transmitting a clue. It's not as if he has his hand in the air waving fingers around conspicuously. All he has to do is casually rest the appropriate number of fingers on his leg. It's a piece of cake.

One finger will indicate the first number in the series; two fingers indicate the second number; and three fingers indicate the last number. This step eliminates the need for Clue #4 (above).

Do you realize what this means? All you have to do is listen for one verbal clue, and then give a quick glance to your partner to determine the exact card that was selected from the deck. Can you imagine the look on everyone's faces when they see you perform this miracle?

Uh-oh. I know what you're thinking. Since I have taken you this far, why stop now? You want me to eliminate the only verbal clue left, don't you? Oh, greedy, greedy reader! Can't you leave well enough alone? Why must you insist on making an already complicated demonstration even more difficult? I don't know what to do with you sometimes. Well, you asked for it . . .

Caution! Do not try this at home!

The one verbal clue that remains tells you the suit of the card by breaking it down to color (black or red) and dominance (spade/heart or club/diamond). You can eliminate the verbal clue if you replace it with the following:

- If the card is black, your partner will have his head tilted slightly. If the card is red, his head will be straight. Are you concerned that you may not be able to recognize a slight tilt? Don't be; it will be obvious to you, but undetectable to the crowd as a clue.
- If the card is a dominant suit (spade or heart), your partner will have his mouth slightly open. If it is a non-dominant suit (club or diamond), his mouth will be closed.

Using this option, your partner does not even have to call you back into the room. He could ask one of the audience members to tell you to return. This way, any suspicion of verbal clues being used will be removed entirely.

Here's a little test: If you walk into the room and see your smiling partner sitting with his right leg over his left, head slightly tilted, mouth closed, three fingers showing in his left hand, what is the card?

Answer:
Head tilted = black card
Mouth closed = Non-dominant suit (club, in this case)
Right leg over left = Top half of the deck (eight through king)
Smiling = Upper three (jack, queen, or king)
Three fingers showing = third card in series (king)
And . . . tada! The card is a king of clubs.

13

Spellbound

DIFFICULTY LEVEL: ✦✦✦✦✦
IMPACT: ✳✳✳✳✳
TECHNIQUE: CODES/PARTNER
PREPARATION: SOME REHEARSAL

Overview

So you like the idea of using codes but hate the thought of learning a complicated system? Then this is a perfect demonstration for you. I modified a well-established mind-reading technique to provide the benefits of using a code without the need to learn complex signals. Although there are similarities between *Spellbound* and *Telepathy for Two*, this code system is much simpler and takes a fraction of the time to master.

The Premise

The mind reader proclaims that his supernatural mental powers are so advanced that he could predict a card that has been selected while he is out of the room. And he will then prove it via this wild demonstration.

The mind reader leaves the room, and the demonstration is conducted by his partner. A deck of cards is produced and the partner asks an audience member to shuffle it thoroughly. As with many other feats described in this book, the spectator should be encouraged to shuffle and cut the deck to his heart's content—shuffle and cut, shuffle and cut *ad nauseum*.

The partner then takes the deck and fans the cards on a table facedown, in clear view of everyone present. Another spectator is asked to select a card and put it aside. Once this is done, the card is shown to everyone in the room (including the partner) and then placed back in the deck.

The mind reader is called back into the room, and miraculously identifies the chosen card.

Solution

As previously mentioned, the solution to this little miracle is a very simple code. Your partner will summon you back into the room and ask the audience to concentrate on the card. Based upon this, you will be able to identify the card.

Here's the code:

There are two elements you must identify: the number of the card and the suit. These two parts will be communicated to you by your partner as follows:

In alphabetical order, the suits are clubs, diamonds, hearts, and spades. Let's number them one through four.

Clubs	=	1
Diamonds	=	2
Hearts	=	3
Spades	=	4

When your partner calls you back into the room, she will signal the suit by the number of words she uses. If the card is a club, she will only use one word (such as "ready!"). If the card is a diamond, then two words will be used. Hearts will be signaled by three words and spades by four.

So if your partner says, "We're all set!", then you know right away that the card must be a heart. Why? Because "We're all set!" is three words, and three words signals a heart.

Even before you walk into the room, you know what the suit is. Let's move on to the number of the card.

There are only thirteen possible answers—ace through king. Each number will be represented by a letter of the alphabet.

For the purpose of this explanation, an ace will be valued as one. Let's match this with the first letter of the alphabet, an "A." The two will be matched with the second letter, a "B." The three will match with a "C" and so forth. When you reach the picture cards, simply convert them into numbers. A jack is an 11, which corresponds with a "K"—the eleventh letter of the alphabet. The queen is matched with the twelfth letter, an "L," and the king is "M" for the thirteenth letter (see chart below).

Ace (1)	=	A
Two	=	B
Three	=	C
Four	=	D
Five	=	E
Six	=	F
Seven	=	G
Eight	=	H
Nine	=	I
Ten	=	J
Jack (11)	=	K
Queen (12)	=	L
King (13)	=	M

What does this all mean? When you return to the room, your partner will ask you to name the card. The first word she says will be the clue you are seeking.

Let's assume that the card is a **nine of clubs.** Well, you already know that the card is a club because your partner only used one word to call you back into the room. But now you need to figure out that it is a nine. According to the above chart, the ninth letter is an "I;" so the very first word spoken by your partner when you return must start with an "I."

How difficult is this? Not at all. There are many words and phrases that begin with the letter "I" that will seem perfectly natural to say. Here are a few examples:

"In a minute, Joe will guess the card."

"I know he will get it."

"Is everyone thinking of the card?"

And that's all! The entire process takes no more than a few seconds, and the code is almost impossible to detect.

Tips & Techniques

Can you believe how easy this code is? This clever system will work every time—especially if you follow the tips and suggestions below.

First, let's discuss the only card that may get you into trouble—the ace. There may be some Einsteins in the audience who will recognize that you are giving a clue that begins with an "A" to indicate an ace. Although this is rare, there is something you can do to throw them off track. Instead of using an "A" word for an ace, just switch it to the fourteenth letter— "N." This way, even the most astute observers will have difficulty deciphering the code. Why the fourteenth letter? Because our code ends with after the thirteenth letter—"M," the clue for king.

There is a tendency to become confused when using codes for jacks and kings. If your partner says, "Just tell us what the card is," she is not indicating a jack for "J," rather a ten because "J" is the tenth letter of the alphabet. Similarly, if you hear your partner say, "Keep concentrating," you should know that "K" stands for the twelfth letter, which is a queen and *not* a king!

Do you think this is confusing? If you study it for a moment, it will become quite clear. Actually, the fact that it is a little perplexing is an advantage for you. Don't you think the audience would catch on if you used a "J" clue for a jack? You don't have to be first in your class at Harvard to realize that the word *keep* just may stand for *king*. It is much better that the clues for jack and king start with letters other than J and K, respectively.

This demonstration, like many others, may work perfectly the first time, but will lose some of its mystique on repeat performances. A nice feature of *Spellbound* is that there are many different clues to use for each letter to keep the audience guessing time and again.

Other Tips

- Another great aspect of this demonstration is that the card is identified so quickly. Within two seconds of re-entering the room, you know the selected card. Once you have deciphered the clues, there is no need to have any contact whatsoever with your partner. In fact, when she is through transmitting your clue, it would be better if she actually left the room. This way no one can accuse her of trying to sneak you the clue through a code. (Imagine such a thing!)

- Since you know the identity of the card within seconds of returning to the room, you have an opportunity to play with your audience. You could walk over to the person who selected the card and hold her hand. Place your other hand on her forehead as if you can sense what the card is from signals being emitted via her brainwaves.

  Do you like music? Well, here's your chance to teach the audience a secret chant to help you identify the card. Or perhaps you'd like to lead them in the *Mind Reading Salsa,* dancing spookily around the room to summon your mystical powers.

  A little too wacky for you? Then maybe you can ask the audience a series of unrelated questions, take a lot of notes, use a calculator (or an abacus if you have one handy), scrape two coins together intensely for an extended period of time, skim through a 1,200-page book (as if the answer is in it), or any other little prank, shenanigan, or spectacle to create the impression that you are setting your powers in motion.

  Once you've had your fill, announce the secret card to the audience.

  In case you need help creating your own clues for each letter of the alphabet, let me get you off to a good start. Remember, we are not using "A" for ace. We're going to match the ace with the fourteenth letter—N. In the following chart, you will notice that most of the clues involve asking the audience to concentrate on the card. This is so that the clues seem more natural and not part of a sneaky, diabolical code.

I am providing two options for each letter. In case you decide to repeat this demonstration over and over, you can vary the clues if the same number should be picked twice.

2   = B = Be quiet.
                Better let him concentrate.

3   = C = Can you all think of the card please?
                Concentrate on the card.

4   = D = Don't distract him.
                Did you think of the card?

5   = E = Everyone concentrate.
                Enough talking.

6   = F = For this part, we need total silence.
                Free your minds of everything but
                   the card.

7   = G = Give him total silence.
                Go for it!

8   = H = He needs total silence.
                Help him by concentrating on the card.

9   = I = I'm going to ask everyone to concentrate
                   on the card.
                Is everyone concentrating on the card?

10   = J = Just concentrate on the card.
                Just give him total silence.

Jack = K = Keep the card in your minds.
                Keep concentrating.

Queen= L = Let's all think of the card
                Let him concentrate.

King = M = Maybe we should all concentrate on
                   the card.
                Mind reading requires concentration.

Ace = N = Now let's all think of the card.
                Nobody talk.

A little practice between you and a trusted friend will make you the hit of any party. Once you master the basic system, you will be able to perform the demonstration flawlessly.

Neighborhood ESP

14

DIFFICULTY LEVEL: ✦✦✦✦✦
IMPACT: ✳✳✳✳✳
TECHNIQUE: PRESET DECK
PREPARATION: MEMORIZATION

Overview

When performed correctly, *Neighborhood ESP* can leave a lasting impression on audiences for weeks and sometimes months after the initial presentation. This feat can only be performed once for a particular audience, so save it for a special occasion.

The Premise

Before beginning, the mind reader asks the host of the party if he could borrow the current edition of a local telephone book. Once this is produced, it is set aside on the table next to a deck of cards.

The mind reader asks a spectator to cut the cards anywhere she pleases. Once she completes the cut, she is instructed to turn over the top two cards and add them together—without showing anyone the cards. For this demonstration, the suits are meaningless. An ace counts as one, jack equals eleven, queen twelve, and king thirteen.

The spectator adds the two cards without announcing the sum. She is then asked to open up the telephone book and turn to the page that corresponds to the total of the two cards. Once she finds the page, the mind reader then asks her to look at the very first entry on the top of the page.

Not only does the mind reader know the name of the first person listed, but he also knows the street address, the town, and the telephone number!

Solution

Do you see what just happened here? The spectator cut the deck *anywhere she pleased*, picked two cards from the top, totaled them, and then opened to the corresponding page in the telephone book. How on earth could you possibly have known the person's name at the top of the page? If this isn't enough to send your audience running for their lives, nothing will.

Your audience will surely be dumbfounded. After all, the deck was cut; it couldn't have been preset! Without seeing the cards, how did you know what the total would be? Theoretically, any two cards could have been drawn with their sum total ranging from two to twenty-six.

Theoretically, that is. In reality, things are quite different. You see, the deck was indeed preset. Because of the way the cards were arranged, there were only two possible sums that could have been calculated—either 14 or 15.

Knowing this, all you have to do is memorize the top listing on both of those pages. And how will you know which page has been selected? Easy: By watching the spectator to see if she looks at the page on the left or on the right. The left page will be an even number (14) while the right page will be odd (15).

Once you identify the correct page, you are able to "read her mind" and treat your audience to a spectacular exhibition of mentalism.

The Setup

Before performing this demonstration, you must preset the deck as follows:

7-8-6-9-5-10-4-J-3-Q-2-K-A-K-2-Q-3-J-4-10-5-9-6-8-7 (repeat)

As you will note, there are only 25 cards listed above. Since you will repeat the order above, the total number of cards that will be used is 50 and not 52. Two of the aces will not make it into this routine. This is no cause for concern.

No matter where the deck is cut, the top two cards will *always* add up to either 14 or 15. Take a look for yourself! No matter which two consecutive cards you select, they will total either 14 or 15. Pretty amazing, don't you think?

You now know the basics of *Neighborhood ESP*. It is time to learn the insider secrets to make this a truly jolting experience for the audience.

Tips & Techniques

Let's start off by discussing the deck itself. This is one of the few demonstrations presented in this book that does not allow the audience to shuffle the cards. Observers are generally quite skeptical about mind reading feats to begin with, and even more so if they are not permitted to shuffle the cards until their hands are numb.

If someone suggests the possibility of the cards being prearranged because no one was given the opportunity to shuffle the deck, you have an effective rebuttal. Although the deck had not been shuffled, *it had been cut.* You could point out to the audience that the spectator had free will to cut the deck anywhere she wanted. You had absolutely no influence on her decision to cut the cards at that precise spot. You could further mention that had she cut the deck at a different point, the total of the cards could very well have been another number. This could only mean that you were using mind reading powers to determine the top listing on the page.

To mislead your audience further, you could actually turn the deck over and show them the cards before the demonstration begins. It will take a person of extraordinary intellect to notice that all of the consecutive cards add up to either 14 or 15. If you do show the audience the cards, this bolsters your argument that you did not tamper with the deck.

If you are still uncomfortable about not letting the audience shuffle the cards, there is another solution. I warn you, it takes a lot of guts. Here goes:

Let the audience have their little shuffle party. Shuffle, shuffle, shuffle. They can spread the cards around the floor and dance on them for all you care; you have a plan. When the audience has finished their shuffling frenzy, they place the cards back on the table.

At this point, you ask the host of the party to bring you his copy of the local telephone book. While he is out of the room, you direct the conversation to other topics. When the audience is distracted, switch the meticulously shuffled deck with the preset second deck you have in your pocket. In any casual setting, you will have ample opportunity to discreetly execute the switch without being detected. The advantage of this method is that you do not have to begin the demonstration until the deck has been switched and you are 100% ready.

Too chicken to pull the old switcheroo? Here is another way to get around the shuffling issue. Perform *Neighborhood ESP* after you have entertained your audience with several other demonstrations. While the audience is reeling over one of your feats of mentalism, watch carefully for an opportunity to switch the deck. Since you just completed a demonstration, the audience has let their collective guard down. There is no reason for them to be suspicious of you now. As far as they are concerned, your performance is over for the evening. Little do they know that you are already plotting your next feat. Again, you are able to take your time and wait as long as necessary to make the switch.

My favorite way of executing this move is by picking up the deck, and in plain view of everyone, completing several full shuffles. This gives the appearance that the cards are being shuffled for the next demonstration. It is a perfectly natural thing to do. While people are wondering how you performed the last demonstration, you are casually mixing up the cards. When the attention is off of you, switch the decks quickly and place the preset cards on the table.

Obviously, the second deck needs to look identical to the first (duh!).

After the fervor from the last demonstration has subsided, suggest to the audience that you try an even more impressive mind reading exercise. Since the deck had just been used in another demonstration, the audience will not think that this is a preset deck that you brought with you. In addition, they did just see you mixing the cards thoroughly only a moment ago. This is generally enough to convince them that you did not manipulate the cards.

Other Tips

- As soon as this demonstration is through, remove the cards from the table and perform a casual shuffle. This is because within 15 seconds of naming the person in the telephone book, it will occur to someone to examine the deck. If you mix the cards—even with one quick shuffle—the pre-arranged order will completely disappear, and the audience will be left without a trace of your evildoing.

  If you shuffle the cards when the demonstration is over, even a full inspection of the deck would not reveal any hanky-panky. If someone were to go as far as counting the cards, he will notice that two cards are missing (the aces you removed earlier); but what will that tell him? Nothing. Ideally, you will switch the decks once again, so that the original cards are back on the table. I realize that this may not be possible, so a quick shuffle will suffice.

- Have you thought about how you will be able to prepare for this demonstration ahead of time? Won't you have to wait to get to your host's home before memorizing the names in his telephone book? Actually, no. If you live close by, you will most likely have the exact same telephone book. Just make sure that it is the current issue. If you do not live in the area, try to stop at a local diner on the way. You can usually find a copy of the current telephone directory.
- There are several pieces of information that you will need to memorize. Besides the name of the persons at the top of pages 14 and 15, you should also remember their street addresses, towns, and telephone numbers. This will make the finish even more remarkable.

Presenting the Finish

Neighborhood ESP provides an opportunity for you to build up to a memorable conclusion. Instead of simply naming the person at the top of the page, work up to it little by little. Close your eyes and use your "mental powers" to think of the person's name and address. The first thing you should do is talk about the house. Mention the type of landscaping around the yard, the number of windows facing the front, the color of the door, and then the types of cars in the driveway.

Of course, the audience will be chuckling, thinking that you are only pretending to know all of these things, but when you mention the town in which the person lives, the laughing will suddenly stop. Now they are on their guard. Of course, still being skeptical, they will assume that this is just a lucky guess. Imagine the look on their faces when you then blurt out the correct address! And then, to top it all off, you announce the name and telephone number as well.

Reputation Builder

There is a way that you can turn this four-star demonstration into an extraordinary feat of supernatural powers that will raise you to the level of mind reader extraordinaire to your friends and family. But like anything else of monumental proportions, it will require more effort on your part.

What I am about to suggest will extend the effect of the demonstration far beyond the initial performance. Assuming that you reside in the general area where you will be performing these demonstrations, chances are that the people listed at the top of pages 14 and 15 will live within a reasonable distance from your home. If this is the case, take a walk or drive to their houses, and make note of the surrounding area.

If you are able to mention the color of the house, the type of street on which the house is situated, the landscaping, the models of cars in the driveway, and even the license plates of the cars, you would be able to carry the demonstration over to the next several days. While the audience is marveling over your uncanny ability to predict the correct name and telephone number, you can suggest that the next time they are in the neighborhood, they should drive by the address that you correctly named to see if the surroundings are accurate.

It is one thing to correctly name a listing in the telephone book, but it is quite another to be able to "envision" the house itself. During the next few days, as your audience has the opportunity to pass by the house in question, they will be startled at the accuracy of your details. Whenever magic tricks or mind reading is brought up in conversation in the future, your name will be mentioned as the person who was able to "see" a stranger's house through sheer mental power. Not a bad reputation!

*J*ndex

Behind the Back 22
  Overview 22
  Premise 22
  Solution 23
  Tips & Techniques 24

How Did I Do That? 41
  Overview 41
  Premise 41
  Solution 43
  Tips & Techniques 44
  Banter 47
  A Great Variation 49

Neighborhood ESP 88
  Overview 88
  Premise 88
  Solution 89
  The Setup 90
  Tips & Techniques 90
  Presenting the Finish 93

One Up 17
  Overview 17
  Premise 17
  Solution 17
  Tips & Techniques 20
  The Shuffle 21
  The List 21

Psychic-in-Training 51
  Overview 51
  Premise 51
  Solution 52
  Tips & Techniques 54

Seven Up 33
  Overview 33
  Premise 33
  The Setup 34
  Solution 34
  Tips & Techniques 35

Spellbound 82
  Overview 82
  Premise 82
  Solution 83
  Tips & Techniques 85
  Other Tips 86

Switcheroo! 56
  Overview 56
  Premise 56
  Solution 57
  Tips & Techniques 59
  Other Tips 61
  Another Version 63

Telepathy for Two 72
  Overview 72
  Premise 72
  Solution 72
  Review 76
  Tips & Techniques 77

The Envelope, Please 29
  Overview 29
  Premise 29
  Solution 30
  Tips & Techniques 30

Under the Table 25
  Overview 25
  Premise 25
  Solution 26
  Tips & Techniques 27
  A Great Finish 28

What's Your Number? 64
  Overview 64
  Premise 65
  Solution 67
  Tips & Techniques 69
  Other Tips 70

About the Author

Author, comedian, magician, puzzle master, and baker of fancy breads, ROBERT MANDELBERG has been perfecting his peculiar brand of mind reading for the past ten years. Many people are afraid to think in his presence, for fear of having their innermost secrets revealed. Just look at him—he's probably reading your mind right now . . . or perhaps he's just recalling a particularly tasty raisin nut loaf.

Because of his overwhelming mind reading ability, Mandelberg's head has actually begun to enlarge to accommodate his ever-expanding brain. "It's not so much his oversized head that I mind," said Mandelberg's wife, Nika. "It's his oversized ego that I find so unbearable."

Mandelberg's other books include *Mystifying Mind Reading Tricks* and *The Case of the Curious Campaign: A Whodunit of Many Mini-Mysteries*. He has performed comedy and magic in colleges, high schools, and nightclubs; and his play, *You're Nobody Until Somebody Kills You,* has been performed throughout the country by the Murder on Cue Mystery Company.

To learn more about Mandelberg's books, performances, and latest tricks and brainteasers, you can visit his website at www.RobertMandelberg.com.